What Everyone Should Know About Business

What Everyone Should Know About Business

A Primer

Patrice Flynn

What Everyone Should Know About Business: A Primer

Interior design by Exeter Premedia Services Private Ltd., Chennai, India

First published in 2019 by
Business Expert Press, LLC
222 East 46th Street, New York, NY 10017
www.businessexpertpress.com

ISBN-13: 978-1-63742-772-9 (paperback)
ISBN-13: 978-1-63742-773-6 (e-book)

Business Expert Press Business Career Development Collection

Second edition: 2025

10 9 8 7 6 5 4 3 2 1

EU SAFETY REPRESENTATIVE
Mare Nostrum Group B.V.
Mauritskade 21D
1091 GC Amsterdam
The Netherlands
gpsr@mare-nostrum.co.uk

ALSO BY PATRICE FLYNN

Introduction to Business:
A Primer on Basic Business Operations

Experiential Learning with Robots:
Teaching New Century University Students in Russia and
the United States Using Autonomous Humanoid Robots

Measuring the Impact of the Nonprofit Sector
(with Virginia Hodgkinson)

Calvert-Henderson Quality of Life Indicators:
A New Tool for Assessing National Trends
(with Hazel Henderson and Jon Lickerman)

Testimonials

Introduction to Business *is a valuable primer on business oper-*
ations in a global economy. It is well written and documented.
It will be useful for anyone interested in business fundamentals."
—The Honorable Ray Marshall, 16th U.S. Secretary of
Labor, Audre and Bernard Rapoport Centennial Chair in
Economics and Public Affairs, and Professor Emeritus at the
University of Texas at Austin

"As a master economics and international studies professor, Dr. Flynn
connects deeply with all of her students—many of whom face per-
sonal challenges and obstacles that could impede their higher educa-
tion experience. Dr. Flynn's capacity to relate to these new-generation
students, as well as her ability to connect theory and practice in
real time, keep every student thoroughly engaged in learning ...
This second edition offers insights into current events in business,
such as breakthroughs in the chips used for generative AI applica-
tions, hyperscale data centers that route global digital internet traf-
fic, and geolocation marketing strategies ... Through her primer,
students are prepared to enter the world of business with confidence
and cutting-edge skills and knowledge as young professionals."
—Laura Wilcox, Former Vice President for Communica-
tions, Council of Independent Colleges

"This small beautifully written paperback text covers the basics with
a personal style aimed at teaching for long-term comprehension ...
Dr. Flynn provides practical insights into how successful companies
started simply and evolved into thriving businesses ... Students will
find this primer an essential guide in their studies and well after
graduation as they navigate the world of operating a successful busi-
ness. It is easily used by nonbusiness professionals to better understand

how businesses work and influence society."—**Thomas H. Powell, President Emeritus of Mount St. Mary's University**

"What Dr. Flynn offers to students learning about the business world is an appreciation of the dynamic and fast-paced world of business … From the trading desks around the world to local nonprofits, everyone can benefit from Dr. Flynn's examination of the functional areas of business."—**Michael J. Driscoll, Ed.D., Senior Managing Director at Bear Stearns, hedge fund Global Head of Trading, former Dean of the Bolte School of Business at Mount St. Mary's University, and Fulbright Specialist**

"What a practical, nonideological, informative book about business; a real how-to from an accomplished educator! I bumbled my way through a small business, but it would have been a lot easier if this book had been available to me back in the day. Given how ubiquitous business is in America, this is a book for everyone: easy to read, easy to understand, and easy to apply. What's not to love about this great little book? If I had a hat, I'd certainly take it off to Professor Patrice Flynn, the number one OG among business educators." —**John J. Flynn III, brother of Patrice Flynn**

"This is a primer for the curious … It allows learners to digest bite-sized pieces of knowledge and encourages them to think freely … Dr. Flynn's pedagogy caters to students of all learning styles, providing the flexibility to adjust teaching methods based on the specific area of business. Real-world case studies not only make it easy for learners to understand and relate to the material but shows how theoretical concepts play out in business scenarios, allowing students to better grasp the relevance and application of what's being studied … Everyone can benefit from learning about the functional areas of business from Dr. Flynn's experience."—**Kaytlin N. Wack, former student and marketer at the Johns Hopkins Federal Credit Union**

"Dr. Flynn's primer offers theoretical and practical information in understandable, conversational language so that anyone without prior

knowledge can jump in and benefit from it … As a distinguished professional and international scholar, Dr. Flynn shares her experience teaching business, economics, and international studies not only from a professor's point of view but also as a business practitioner. Her expertise in the classroom is excellently translated into written form … Generation Z has grown up in a world where opportunities are endless. They quickly adapt to the need to evaluate and sift through huge amounts of information. They also shy away from lengthy, expensive business textbooks. Thus, this primer definitely meets their needs."
—**Irina L. Pervova, PhD, Professor of Psychology and Social Work at Saint-Petersburg State University, Russia**

"Dr. Patrice Flynn's textbook is direct and to the point … Her teaching style makes sure that all of her students know core business definitions and concepts forward and backward before moving on. As a result, I can remember more content longer and more easily than from other college courses. I often go back to my notes from her course and notes I took from the textbook to make sure I have the basics right. Dr. Flynn's A Primer is the perfect book to accompany students on their journey."—**Abigail Finafrock, student at Mount St. Mary's University**

"This is a unique primer that provides students with essential information about business in our current complex and global environment. Author Patrice Flynn, PhD, a veteran business professor with decades of executive experience in the business private sector, provides up-to-date information with real and relatable examples. The text's conversational tone skillfully invites students to exercise imagination and personal reflection. For educators, the topics can be flexibly arranged in any order to align with course and learning outcomes, customizing the rich content to students' needs. This is a 'must' for students in any academic major who seek to explore their place in the modern business world."—**Carol Z. Rinkoff, PhD, former Dean of the Frederick Campus of Mount St. Mary's University; Dean of Academic Affairs, Pacific Oaks College; and Vice President of Academic Affairs, Argosy University**

Contents

Preface

In your hands is a unique and timely student-driven product with the following key characteristics.

- This is a **primer** (pronounced prɪmər), not a lengthy and expensive textbook. Primers present the core elements of a subject to prepare a targeted audience for what comes next.
- This primer presents the **functional areas of business**, a term used by businesspeople to identify the key topics that all businesses must understand to be successful (e.g., entrepreneurship, small business development, economic competition, legal structure, growth strategies, global business, finance, digitization, marketing, and management).
- This primer helps college and university students decide what aspects of business might be of greatest interest to them. My hope is that students utilize this text to advance their academic performance and subsequent career decisions.

What else distinguishes this business primer from contemporary textbooks?

- The content will aid entrepreneurs as they design their own businesses, even if they've never taken a course in a business school.
- This primer integrates **global business** into every functional area of business. No matter where we live, our businesses are impacted by globalization in some manner. It no longer suffices to teach business fundamentals without a comprehensive presentation on

how to globalize a business. As a veteran educator of modern business and a business owner, I believe that students no longer have the luxury of not thinking globally. Any successful business today will require some knowledge of the global nature of our work.

- The style incorporates feedback received from more than 2,000 undergraduate students I have taught live and in-person over the past 15 years.
- The text is written in the **second person** to personalize learning and engage readers who are interested in working for a business one day or starting their own business.
- The tone is **conversational** to capture the imaginations of students and to model the idea that learning is an interpersonal endeavor.
- This primer assumes **no prior knowledge** of the *functional areas of business*; hence, anyone can jump in and benefit from the teachings.
- The material is accessible to business majors as well as **nonbusiness majors** interested in understanding the world of business before graduating from university.
- In addition to my role as professor of business, economics, and international studies, I am a **businesswoman,** who for 20 years served as senior vice president for administration and finance and then chief executive officer (CEO) in the private business sector, where I had direct experience implementing each of the *functional areas of business* presented in this primer. Students value my firsthand experience and candor regarding business practicalities as well as my ability to discern and sort through what is most important for students to understand.
- This primer brings to light cutting-edge business practices, leaving behind outdated concepts.
- This primer is **not a polemic**. I have no agenda here. The key *functional areas of business* are presented

without judgment or prejudice. I want readers to understand how business is conducted—plain and simple—and to determine on their own accord which functional areas of business most interest them and why.

Business Expert Press offers this 2nd edition because business is never static. Updated statistics provide important insights on the latest number, receipts, and net income of legal businesses in the United States; rankings on the largest businesses worldwide; the survival rates and characteristics of new businesses; and notable trends in the financing of businesses today.

In addition, this edition provides new business examples and case studies to include the growing presence of: limited partnerships, limited liability corporations, and private equity firms; the impact of digitization on global businesses; entrepreneurial interest in hyperscale data centers and microchips that power artificial intelligence applications; the use of data analytics in merchandising; and more.

Career Guide

Some say the perfect baseball player possesses five tools to become a star: running, throwing, fielding, hitting, and hitting for power. Legendary baseball player Mays (1931–2024) possessed all five, becoming one of the greatest players who ever lived.

The equivalent in business is what we call the *functional areas of business*. These are the key domains or fields of study required to understand how businesses are established, run, and grow. Examples of the functional areas of business include entrepreneurship, small business development, legal structure, economic competition, growth strategies, going global, finance, digitization, marketing, and management, each explored in this primer.

Part of my job as a professor at a liberal arts university is to help advise business students. My advice is not limited to academic goals. If a student is willing, I am available to provide career and workplace guidance. I think I have been successful in guiding advisees and would like to believe that I could do the same thing on a larger scale through this primer.

At the end of this primer, not only will every student come away with a sense of one or two business areas that pique their interests and could be pursued in subsequent semesters, but students will also be grounded in the *functional areas of business*. Regardless of which area of business one ultimately pursues, it is imperative that everyone who works in business grasps what a business is and how business is operationalized through the functional areas in the context of contemporary global capitalism.

My years of teaching the *functional areas of business* has taught me that **business and nonbusiness majors** benefit from learning about business fundamentals. Majors in biology, psychology, theology, philosophy, history, health and environmental sciences, music, education, performing arts, international studies, world languages, political science, accounting, finance, criminal justice, sociology, sport management, information systems, veteran affairs, and computer science sign up for my course. Having nonbusiness students in the mix enriches our conversations and provides me with new insights into the value of studying contemporary business practices.

Students express a desire to graduate from college knowing a little about business because they recognize that we live and work in a global world. I wholeheartedly agree and welcome all students to join me in an exciting adventure exploring the nature of business as we experience it in today's global economy, a subject I find endlessly fascinating!

Primer Structure

This primer provides professors with the right amount of information needed for an introductory one-semester business course. There is no need for a teaching edition of this textbook because

I see teachers and students as collaborators in the classroom, as we explore business in real time.

The primer is organized into 12 chapters, each a stand-alone document, corresponding to approximately one week of classroom time when supplemented with real-time business examples.

> Chapter 1 defines the commonly used terms *business* and *functional areas of business*, hence grounding students in the material to be examined in each subsequent chapter.
>
> Chapter 2 examines the broader economy in which businesses operates and how that impacts both competition and our decision making.
>
> Chapter 3 lays out three main business legal structures for students to consider when establishing a new business: sole proprietorships, partnerships, and corporations.
>
> Chapter 4 explores ways that a business can grow domestically.
>
> Chapter 5 considers options for how a business can go global with and without leaving home.
>
> Chapter 6 captures the essence of entrepreneurship and small business development.
>
> Chapters 7 through 9 explore the financial functional area of business, beginning with financial management, then equity finance and debt finance.
>
> Chapters 10 and 11 focus on the areas of digitization, marketing, and public relations, all rapidly changing fields of study.
>
> Chapter 12 concludes with business management, including the roles and functions required of effective managers, using all the new skills and knowledge on the functional areas of business learned in this book.

When teaching the functional area of business, I incorporate decision-making exercises to give students opportunities to consider how businesspeople solve problems and make critical decisions on a day-to-day basis across the functional areas. This approach encourages students to treat decision making as a process that invites them to stop, think, observe, diagnose, and focus on content. Critical thinking becomes integral when coupled with the analytical problem-solving methodology commonly used in business settings.

Lastly, to professors who are teaching a course on the *functional areas of business*, feel free to present this material in your courses in any order that suits your teaching style and student body. Each chapter can be inserted into your course curriculum as needed. The business statistics and cases reflect state-of-the art information as this primer goes to press.

I wholeheartedly encourage you to find creative ways to interject your own insights on best practices as they continue to unfold in the ever-changing and exciting world of global business!

CHAPTER 1

The Functional Areas of Business

A valuable starting point for anyone interested in learning about business is the examination of the *functional areas of business*, a term used by businesspeople to describe the key domains that all businesses must focus on to be successful. Some of the functional areas of business include entrepreneurship, small business development, legal structure, finance, growth strategies, going global, digitization, marketing, and management.

Ultimately, if you are going to work in business, you must decide which *functional area of business* most closely matches your interests, skills, and knowledge. How do you know what aspects of business suit you best? What business courses should you take to pursue your interests? Students tell me their usual approach is to look at the college course catalog and make selections based on a course title or a descriptive sentence. Given the exorbitant cost of college today, this is an expensive and sometimes futile method of course selection, much less career exploration. This primer provides a solution to such a guessing game.

The information in this primer serves as a guide for college students who are contemplating going into the field of business and are not sure what courses to take. With the aid of this primer, students will be grounded in the *functional areas of business*. Students will come away with a sense of one or two functional areas that pique their interest and could be pursued in subsequent semesters.

In addition, students recognize that we all live and work in a global capitalist economy and might therefore benefit from studying the essence of business thinking and operations. Knowing the fundamentals of business helps us make more informed decisions in our daily capacities as (a) consumers of business products and services; (b) recipients of microtargeting and other forms of merchandising; (c) users of financial instruments; and (d) workers who report to a boss. Thus, I welcome business and nonbusiness students to use this primer to help navigate today's global economy, a subject that captures my imagination each day.

We'll start by giving meaning to the terms *business* and *functional areas of business*.

What Is a Business?

We hear and use the term *business* often in daily conversation. We tell friends of our interest in studying business. We stream the nightly business news. We read the business section of newspapers. We follow business online news feeds. Business executives are regularly interviewed on mass media by journalists.

What Is a Business?

An organization
comprised of people
who produce goods and services
to sell
to earn a profit
distributed to stakeholders.

What is a business? Simply put, a business is an organization comprised of people who produce goods and services to sell to customers, with the expectation of earning a profit to be distributed to stakeholders.

The business **organization** is our unit of analysis. An organization:

- Can be large or small;
- Can have any number of employees, from one to thousands;
- Can operate a single store or 10,000 stores;
- Can produce goods and services in any of the industries tracked by the U.S. Department of Labor; and
- Can employ workers from the hundreds of different occupations represented in the modern workforce.

The various types of business organizational structures in the United States provide the legal framework for commercial activities, as explored in Chapter 3.

A business is an organization comprised of **people** who are employed to help the entity achieve its goals. These people come from all different occupational and industrial backgrounds. Their levels of education vary from job to job as do the roles and functions performed for the business. Some people are employed as wage and salary workers, others as contractors, sole proprietors, or self-employed persons. As will be stressed in Chapter 12 on management, people make the business. If you are a people-person, you probably will do well in business. You may even choose to study human resource management or international management, which are specializations in business management.

What are the people who work in a business organization doing all day? They **produce products or provide services** that are unique to their business enterprise. Economists identify two types of products. The first is called "goods," which represent tangible items produced for sale to customers (e.g., robots, microchips, mobile devices, shoes). The second is called "services," which represent other products offered to customers (e.g., plumbing, roofing repairs, physical therapy, language translation, computer–brain interface surgery). As presented in Chapter 6, entrepreneurship is central to taking an idea and making it a reality.

The products produced by a business are intended to be **sold** to existing or new customers. This is where workers skilled in sales, advertising, and merchandising come into the picture. As we all know, the job of a salesperson in the 2020s contrasts starkly with a sales job in the 20th century due to the advent of electronic sales on networked digital platforms, known as ecommerce. If becoming a salesperson is of interest to you, take a careful look at Chapters 10 and 11 on digitization and marketing to get a jump on this functional area of business.

The process of hiring people to produce products and services to be sold to customers is intended to earn the owners of the business a **profit**, defined as total revenues minus total costs. By definition, private for-profit businesses are in the business of making money, which is what differentiates business from the two other sectors of the U.S. economy: (a) the public sector and (b) the private nonprofit sector.

If profit is your goal, the private for-profit business sector is where you belong. For-profit firms strive to find appropriate ways to grow their businesses and hence increase profits, as considered in Chapters 4 and 5. Financial mechanisms to secure adequate financing for such growth are explored in Chapters 7, 8, and 9.

Lastly, who gets to keep the profits earned by a business? By law, the profits are **distributed to the stakeholders** on record. As discussed in Chapter 3 on business structure, businesses that are set up as sole proprietors distribute profits to the single owner of the business. Those set up as partnerships distribute profits to the general or limited partners per the partnership agreement. Businesses set up as corporations have a fiduciary responsibility to distribute profits to all owners, including shareholders.

Examples of the Functional Areas of Business

Now that we have a clear definition of a business, let's look at some of the key functional areas of business. In this primer, the functional areas presented do not include all functional areas, but rather those my students and I have identified as the most valuable in the initial stages of considering a career in business. The functions presented will help you understand what is required to start and run a successful business.

Entrepreneurship and Small Business Development

Entrepreneurship is where business begins and may lead to the establishment of a new legal business entity. Small business development stems from an initial idea and develops into the design of a business plan, consultation with attorneys, registering the new entity with the U.S. Internal Revenue Service (IRS, if operating in the United States), and the establishment of operations.

For some students, owning and operating their own business is the goal. For others, finding an established business in need of one's skills and knowledge is the goal. In either case, it is valuable to understand the entrepreneurial nature of the business as envisioned by the person who created the enterprise and/or those who hold the responsibility for running the business day-to-day.

Finance

The securing, handling, and distribution of money is a central functional area for all businesses and requires in-depth knowledge of finance and accounting. Most business programs include courses in accounting to give students a grounding in best practices to account for financial flows, adhere to generally agreed-upon accounting practices, and disseminate financial information to stakeholders. Financial management entails establishing clear financial goals with business owners, drafting a budget, and securing financing, if needed. Both equity financing and debt financing options are potential sources of money to create, build, and grow a business.

Everyone entrusted with running a business, whether a business owner or an employee, benefits from understanding the financial and accounting functional areas of the firm.

Digitization

A new functional area of business introduced in the 21st century is digitization, known also as data science, data analytics, or behavioral futures markets. With the advent of sophisticated computational hardware, software, and connectivity, businesses today control enormous virtual supply chains of behavioral data on customer preferences, emotions, purchases, lifestyles, interests, and more. Merchandisers have found ways to monetize these data for the benefit of the world's advertisers and others who pay for its prediction products that retain and attract more customers.

Data insights build on the genius of the Ad Men and Ad Women of the 20th century and bring new meaning to merchandising. If you are interested in merchandising, the digitization functional area is the best starting place for your studies.

Marketing and Public Relations

In addition to digitization, merchandisers learn how to harness the four marketing Ps, namely: place, product, price, and promotion to increase sales, revenues, and profits for the firm. Options for novel places to sell products have exploded due to people carrying devices that allow marketers to microtarget products directly to potential customers, regardless of where the person and the products are physically located. Increasingly, data brokers will engage in behavioral modification to nudge us toward certain decisions and actions. It is predicted that soon there will be no price tags on merchandise or store shelves as AI-powered microchip sensors and software will generate a unique price for each customer to be posted on the person's mobile device.

Unique pricing is made possible through digitization, handheld devices, beacons, microchips, and predictive analysis, all of which you will study in your marketing courses. The vice presidents for public relations have their work cut out for them in today's 24/7 news cycle environment that demands increasing communication between business and society.

Going Global

The world of business has also changed significantly as business-people expand their geographical purview to include all corners of the globe. Financing, for example, is no longer limited to the country in which a business is incorporated. The workforce is no longer limited to a local economy, as workers migrate across state and national borders. The supply of inputs to production moves across the six inhabited continents. Potential customers of your products and services may live anywhere on Earth.

Today, 195 sovereign nations engage in $24 trillion worth of merchandise trade flows and $7.5 trillion worth of commercial service flows annually. Gross global production is valued at $100 trillion. As more and more businesses enter the global business arena, earth-shattering global supply chains and infrastructure systems are constructed that defy traditional notions of operations and logistics.

In this primer, I argue that readers no longer have the luxury of limiting their view of business to a single domestic economy. We all are best served by understanding the global interconnections of contemporary commerce. Hence, going global is a vital functional area of the firm to help your business grow and prosper.

Management

Last but not least, management has and always will be a central functional area of business given the all-important role that people play in reaching business goals. Human resource specialists examine the educational backgrounds, skills, and knowledge workers acquired over their work lives and try to match those abilities with the needs of business. Labor contracts, wages, compensation, expectations, and performance are examined in this functional area.

Every manager benefits from learning how to facilitate the ongoing process of harnessing and guiding people and other resources to achieve specific business goals. If you choose to take specialized business management courses, you will learn how to be an effective manager vis-à-vis the functions and roles you play as a manager.

Wrap Up

This chapter represents some of the key aspects of business that every businessperson needs to understand to appreciate the comprehensiveness of what we call *business*. While not all *functional areas of business* are covered in this primer, students will come away with a solid understanding of the key functional areas that will help guide their careers and future course of study.

CHAPTER 2

Business and the Economy

The United States is the largest economy in the world. In 2024, the Bureau of Economic Analysis reported that gross domestic product—the value of all final U.S. goods and services produced—topped $28 trillion. The only country that comes close to this figure is the People's Republic of China, with an $18-trillion economy.

Every aspect of business is impacted by the economy in which we operate. Thus, it is valuable to understand the size and scope of the domestic economy and how economic factors might impact your business.

In the following, we will explore two key concepts to help you consider how your business fits into the economy: (1) the competitiveness continuum and (2) the business cycle.

Competitiveness Continuum

There are hundreds of industries in the United States, from automobiles to data platforms, insurance, education, oil and gas, real estate, finance, construction, textiles, steel, medicine, and more. The best place to begin your job quest is to decide which industry captures your interest. This is a personal decision that will require research on what you can expect to be doing if you pursue a job and/or start a business in a particular industry.

Once you have homed in on a particular industry, the next thing to explore is the degree of competition within that industry. **Competition** is a central theme in business and is embraced by businesspeople on the road to success. A risk-averse person may not find success in business, but a person who thrives on competition will likely succeed.

Before you launch your new business or go to a job interview, examine where your industry fits on the competitiveness continuum.

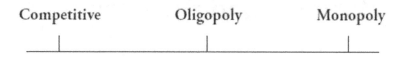

Competitive   Oligopoly   Monopoly

Competitive Industries

On the far left of the competitiveness continuum are the highly competitive industries with an array of business activities, featuring numerous producers and sellers. Competition at this end of the continuum is intense; to succeed, these businesses must ensure a wide variety of choices for consumers.

Monopolistic Industries

In contrast, on the far right of the competitiveness continuum are industries with little to no competition. When one business dominates an industry, this is referred to as a **monopoly**.

In the 20th century, the United States saw the rise of three monopolistic industries. Case one was **Standard Oil**, founded by John D. Rockefeller, which faced national scrutiny for being a monopolist in the crude-oil industry and was forced to break up in 1911. The second case was the breakup of **AT&T** (American Telephone & Telegraph) in 1984 for exhibiting monopoly power in the communications industry. The third landmark case arose when **Microsoft** was deemed by the U.S. Department of Justice (DOJ) as a monopoly in the computer industry in 1999 and forced to allow non-Microsoft browsers to run on its operating system.

Talk of modern-day anticompetitive behavior revolves around Silicon Valley digital platforms. **Apple**, for example, has been accused of breaking European Union (EU) rules on fair competition under the EU's 2022 Digital Markets Act (DMA) designed to help small businesses by requiring online "gatekeepers"—most of whom are U.S. businesses—to run their platforms fairly and to open up their businesses to competition or face hefty fines. Specifically, the EU accused Apple of placing restrictions on how its two million app developers can sell to their customers on Apple's App Store. If found guilty of breaking the gatekeeper rules, Apple would have to pay a penalty of 10 percent of its global annual revenue. For repeat offences, the fine could rise to 20 percent.

Microsoft has also been accused by the EU of exercising monopoly power by bundling its team's videoconferencing app software with its Office suite. Competing video conference providers reported anticompetitive behavior to Margrethe Vestager, the EU's executive vice president in charge of competition policy. Vestager said, "We are dealing with the biggest and most valuable companies on the planet. The DMA is not an excessive ask. It is plain vanilla to ask for a fair, open and contestable marketplace" (FT 2024).

Similar anticompetitive practices are being examined in the United States. In 2023, the U.S. Federal Trade Commission and 17 state's Attorney Generals sued Amazon for operating a monopoly by using its power to raise prices and degrade service for shoppers and vendors while stifling competition. A trial date is set for October 2026.

Also in 2023, 50 state's Attorney Generals, plus Washington DC and Puerto Rico, brought a monopoly case to the U.S. Government on behalf of software makers who sell their products on **Google Play Store**. Google's policy was such that if a customer downloaded an app from Google's Play Store for $100, Google would keep $30 and the app maker would get $70. Right before the case was set to go to trial at the U.S. DOJ in November 2023, Google settled, agreeing to allow software makers who sell through the Google Play Store to charge customers directly.

But that is not the end of the story. On August 5, 2024, the U.S. DOJ ruled—in an historic trial—that **Google is an illegal**

monopoly in the general search engine industry. This is a foundational decision in American law. Judge Amit Mehta wrote, "After having carefully considered and weighed the witness testimony and evidence, the court reaches the following conclusion: Google is a monopolist, and it has acted as one to maintain its monopoly. It has violated Section 2 of the Sherman Act."*

Google successfully created a monopoly whereby 90% of all U.S. internet search queries pass through its search engine (95% for mobile devices). The U.S. Department of Justice said the "remedy phase" to fix the problems identified in the trial were expected to begin immediately.

Oligopolistic Industries

In the middle of the competitiveness continuum is a set of industries where only a few businesses operate, known as **oligopolies**. Examples of U.S.-registered oligopolistic industries include automobiles (General Motors and Ford), pharmaceuticals (Eli Lilly, Novo Nordisk, Johnson & Johnson, and Merck), wireless carriers (Verizon, T-Mobile US, and AT&T), car rentals (Enterprise, Avis Budget, and Hertz), soft drinks (Coca-Cola and Pepsi), airline manufacturing (Boeing and Airbus), health insurance (e.g., Kaiser Permanente, Elevance Health (Anthem), HCSC, and United Health Group), and mobile phones (e.g., Apple's iPhone and Google's Android).

In sum, knowing the competitive nature of the industry in which you plan to work or start a business is key to success.

---

* See United States of America vs Google LLC. August 5, 2024. "Case No. 20-cv- 3010 (APM)." www.courtlistener.com/docket/18552824/1033/united-states-of-america-v-google-llc/.

One of the biggest changes regarding the competitiveness continuum in the United States during the first half of the 21st century is the growing concentration of businesses within industries, making it difficult for small business owners to break into selected industries. Specifically, we see fewer industries exhibiting competitiveness and more industries exhibiting oligopolistic-cum-monopolistic traits.

Business Cycle

Businesspeople track an array of key economic indicators from which to assess their own well-being in the context of the larger economy in which we conduct business. One such economic indicator is known as the business cycle, representing the ebbs and flows of a nation's economy.

The business cycle is divided into four parts: **expansion, peak, contraction,** and **trough**. An expansion is when an economy is experiencing an upswing during which we would expect to see rising output, income, employment, industrial production, and wholesale–retail sales. The peak is when an economy reaches a relative high before moving into a contraction, or downturn, with an expected drop in output, income, and employment. The trough is a relative low in the business cycle, indicating a turn from a contraction into an expansionary period.

The entity entrusted with tracking the U.S. business cycle is the National Bureau of Economic Research (NBER), a nonprofit organization established in 1920 in Cambridge, Massachusetts. Its charge is to carefully examine myriad data on the U.S. economy and determine where the economy is located on the business cycle.

The NBER's most recent announcement on the business cycle indicated that the last peak occurred in February 2020 and the last trough was in April 2020. NBER concluded that the contraction between these two months was "so great and so widely diffused throughout the economy that, even if it proved to be quite brief, the downturn should be classified as a recession, the shortest ever in the US" (July 19, 2021).

Becoming aware of where the United States stands in the business cycle is critical for business success. Choosing to open your business at a time when the economy is shifting from a peak into a contraction could yield different results than opening a business when the economy is shifting from a trough into an expansion.

Moreover, how a business responds to changes in the business cycle depends on its industry. Some industries may perform poorly during contractions (e.g., restaurants) relative to other industries that may perform better during contractions (e.g., grocery stores), depending on the needs of consumers and their disposable income. Become aware of the preferences and behaviors of customers in your industry in anticipation of business cycle fluctuations.

Wrap Up

Context is everything. While you will do all within your power to ensure that your business is a success, there will be times when the larger forces of an economy dominate your decision-making capabilities. For this reason, it helps to know a bit about the economy in which your business operates to understand aggregate economic trends as it impacts your success. A good starting place is to become familiar with the competitiveness continuum and business cycle, the focus of most daily business news feeds.

CHAPTER 3

Business Legal Structure

Once you gain a sense of the larger economy in which businesses operate and have a clear understanding of where your industry sits on the competitiveness continuum, it is time to decide how to set up your business. This is a legal matter that hinges upon the laws in whatever nation and state you want to conduct business.

Structure is captured in the first part of our answer to the question, "What is a business?" Specifically, business begins with the establishment of a particular **organizational type** or **legal structure**. To help you consider which business structure might best suit your needs, this chapter presents the major business types in the United States: sole proprietorships, partnerships, and corporations.

What Is a Business?

An organization
comprised of people
who produce goods and services
to sell
to earn a profit
distributed to stakeholders

You already made an important choice vis-à-vis organizational structure when you decided to create a private for-profit business as opposed to a public-sector agency or a private non-profit organization. Within each of these three sectors of our economy, the kinds of entities that are legally permitted vary considerably. In the public sector, for example, a variety of governmental entities exist at the national, state, city, and municipal levels. In the private nonprofit sector, the U.S. IRS ascribes 35 types of nonprofit entities.

Choices within the private for-profit business sector are somewhat simpler, with three basic forms, specifically **sole proprietorships**, **partnerships**, and **corporations**, each of which is described as follows, followed by a discussion of their relative size and advantages.

The choice of business structure depends on your specific industry, business model, and financial goals. If you plan to own, operate, and finance your business without external influence, you will likely establish your firm as a sole proprietorship, which is the most common type of business in the United States based on the number of business entities registered with the IRS. If you want to own, run, and finance your business with other people, a partnership may be most suitable. If you are seeking to ultimately sell your business or grow to a size whereby most of the functional areas will be run by hired employees or subcontractors, you most likely will want to consider establishing your business as a corporation.

Initially, do not be overly concerned about choosing just the right type of organizational structure for your business. U.S. law is such that you may change your legal business type if you deem it valuable over time, one of the reasons we like to conduct business in the United States!

Type 1: Sole Proprietorships

Imagine watching an old spaghetti Western movie in which someone walks into a saloon and demands to speak to the proprietor of this establishment. With whom does the person want to speak? Historically, the answer is the owner of the saloon, who is entrusted with making most if not all of the decisions regarding this particular establishment.

We do not usually hear people use the old 17th-century English term *proprietor* any longer. In modern times, if a person wants to speak to someone who can help with a problem at a particular business establishment, one asks to speak to either the manager or the supervisor on duty.

The term *sole proprietor*, although linguistically outdated, is still used to identify a specific type of business for legal purposes. The term *sole* suggests that there is one owner of the business. The term *proprietor* refers to the person in charge of the business, in this case the owner. Hence, sole proprietorships are businesses owned and operated by a single person who has full responsibility for business activities and outcomes. The sole proprietorship exists until the owner shutters the business or dies.

Some sole proprietorships begin as a small business easily managed by a single person, but over time may grow into large enterprises that require rethinking the legal structure of the business. Consider the individual named **Sam Walton**, who first learned the retail trade when he bought a franchise license in 1945 and successfully operated a Ben Franklin variety store in Newport, Arkansas. Walton parlayed his newly honed skills into his own store in Bentonville, Arkansas, called the Walton's Five and Dime that opened on May 9, 1950. Twelve years later, Walton owned and operated 16 retail stores and decided to open what he called the Walmart Discount City store in Rogers, Arkansas, on July 2, 1962, thus forging his unique one-stop retail business model that fundamentally changed commerce in rural and suburban America.

Over time, Sam Walton became the primary stakeholder in the largest retail corporation in the world, Walmart Inc. By the time of his death in 1992, there were 1,960 Walmart stores worldwide, a number that has since risen to 10,500 in 19 countries.

Think also about the cartoon artist named **Walt Disney**, who drew cartoons in his garage in Kansas City, Missouri, a space shared with a mouse who inspired a famed Disney character. Disney first began to achieve modest success after teaming up with his business-minded brother, Roy, to form the Walt Disney Company in Los Angeles, California, on October 16, 1923. Since those early days, the sole proprietorship transformed into the Disney Brothers Cartoon Studio in 1928, with Walt and Roy as equal partners, and ultimately the world's largest entertainment empire, the Walt Disney Company, long outliving the Disney brothers.

Think about the man named **Henry Ford**, who was a machinist and engineer working in Detroit, Michigan, in the years leading up to the advent of the automobile. To distinguish himself, Ford built a "Quadricycle," a gasoline-powered horseless carriage in the shed behind his home in 1896.

Seven years later, he established the Ford Motor Company, made famous by operationalizing Frederick Taylor's assembly line, a mass production process that reduced the time it took to assemble one Model T from 12 hours to 90 minutes. His business persisted despite the drop in the number of U.S. carmakers from some 500 in 1900 to 200 in 1908.

Henry Ford's business is now a global automotive enterprise led by Henry Ford's great-grandson, William Clay Ford Jr., executive chair of the Ford Motor Company, one of only two remaining U.S.-owned carmakers. The Ford Motor Company continued to demonstrate its ability to withstand the forces of global capitalism. In the depths of the Great Recession, Ford's stock price hit a low of $1.01 on November 20, 2008. By 2023, its profit rose to $10 billion on $176 billion in revenues and closed the year with a stock price of $12.19.

As the Ford Motor Company and others illustrate, just because you start your business as a sole proprietorship does not mean you must retain this type of business structure forever. History reveals many cases of small business owners whose sole proprietorships grew to become either partnerships, corporations, and/or transcontinental national corporations. In the United States, it is fairly easy to change your business structure if that is desirable to meet your operational needs and long-term vision.

Sole proprietorships operate across a variety of industries, including restaurants, bakeries, gift shops, retail stores, professional services, family-owned farms, and more. In fact, of the 115 industries the U.S. Department of Labor's Bureau of Labor Statistics (BLS) has tracked since the 1930s, most have been dominated by sole proprietorships, at least when initially created.

The BLS classifies each business into the industry in which it is primarily engaged, alongside establishments doing similar things in similar ways. The North American Industry Classification System (NAICS) changes as new industries emerge over time, most recently cybersecurity, forensic accounting, and data science.

The current NAICS coding structure, introduced in 1997, classifies economic activity into 20 major industrial sectors.

- Five sectors are goods-producing enterprises (i.e., natural resources; agriculture, fishing, forestry, and hunting; mining, quarrying, oil and gas extraction; construction; and manufacturing).
- Fifteen sectors are service-providing enterprises (i.e., wholesale trade; retail trade; transportation and warehousing; utilities; information; finance and insurance; real estate and rental and leasing; professional, scientific, and technical services;

management of companies and enterprises; administrative and support and waste management and remediation services; education and health services; health care and social assistance; arts, entertainment, and recreation; accommodation and food services; and all other services).

Statistics on Sole Proprietorships

How many sole proprietorships are there in the United States and how much money do these businesses bring in? Up-to-date statistics on business activities are published on a regular basis by the U.S. IRS. The IRS collects data each year directly from private for-profit businesses, then verifies, collates, and releases the numbers in the *Statistics of Income (SOI) Bulletin* every quarter (winter, spring, summer, and fall). Because the most recent data are provided on a rolling basis from active, registered businesses, the IRS continuously updates the official data counts. Thus, do not be surprised if you see differences in initially released statistics and later bulletins.

The SOI statistical data collection effort dates back to 1916, providing us with more than a century of historical data on business activities in the United States by type of entity. For our purposes, we will examine three key pieces of information that are regularly reported in the *SOI Bulletins*: the number of business entities by type that are registered with the IRS, the annual receipts of these entities in U.S. dollars, and the annual net income in U.S. dollars (see www.IRS.gov/taxstats).

Table 3.1 Statistics on sole proprietorships

Number of Entities	29,309,600
Receipts (USD)	$1.9 trillion
Net Income (USD)	$411 billion

Source: IRS. SOI Bulletin: Summer 2024.

Table 3.1 presents a summary of the most recent data available on sole proprietorships in the United States. Notable is the fact that there are more than 29 million sole proprietorships registered with the U.S. IRS that have the legal right to conduct business in the United States. These businesses brought in $1.9 trillion in receipts through the production and sale of goods and/or services. After all vendors, employees, and others who are owed money were paid, sole proprietors netted $411 billion, a handsome profit.

Why Start Your Business as a Sole Proprietorship?

Given that more than 29 million businesspeople chose to start their businesses as sole proprietorships, it is worthwhile to examine some of the advantages and disadvantages of running a sole proprietorship.

One of the key benefits of a sole proprietorship is that it is **easy to start**, relative to other business types. You do not need to hire (and pay) an attorney to legally set up your sole proprietorship, although this option is available if you like. You can learn how to register your business with the IRS by yourself, hence, saving money and time immediately. It is also quite easy to obtain a license (or permit) to conduct business in your state, as required by law.

Even if you do not want to register your business with the IRS, you can still conduct business in the United States. By default, the IRS will treat any income (and loss) attributed to your commercial activities as it does for registered sole proprietorships.

Moreover, sole proprietorships do not require charters or registration with the secretary of state in the state where you conduct business.

Sole proprietorships are **inexpensive to start** as you have the option of starting small (i.e., small inventory, small or no paid staff, and no lawyers). Sole proprietorships are also **easy to close** should you decide at some point that business is not the career path for you. All you are required to do is send a letter to the IRS with notification that you are no longer going to be in business as of a specified date. Of course, you cannot walk away from any outstanding obligations or debts, the latter of which must be paid even if you shutter your business, as will be discussed in the chapter on debt financing.

Those who decide to establish a business as a sole proprietorship also benefit from the privileges accorded to the business owner. For example, you get to make all the decisions, a benefit that may be one of the main reasons you are going into business in the first place. You also get to keep all the profits, once suppliers and all other stakeholders are paid, of course. With sole proprietors, there are no partners who will demand a cut of the profits.

One other advantage of owning a sole proprietorship is the **ease of reporting earnings and paying taxes** to the IRS. Sole proprietors are required to report to the IRS their business revenues, expenditures, net income, and/or losses by April 15th of each year. These data are reported on the standard U.S. Individual Income Tax Return, IRS Form 1040, which every adult in the United States must complete and submit annually.

On the IRS Form 1040, sole proprietors report "Business income (or loss)" and attach details of business revenues and expenditures for the year on Schedule C (or C-EZ). There are no additional IRS forms to be completed, making annual tax filings straightforward for owners of sole proprietorships.

This easy way to file taxes for sole proprietorships reflects the U.S. ethos of supporting small businesses and facilitating smooth operations a business easy. By allowing business owners to report business income (or loss) directly on the IRS Form 1040, the income is treated as a "passthrough," meaning there are no additional business taxes owed to the U.S. Department of the Treasury, such as corporate income taxes that must be paid by businesses legally established as corporations as discussed below. Business profits are taxed at the individual person's personal tax bracket such as wage and salary income.

Downsides of Sole Proprietorships

There are several disadvantages to be aware of if you are going to establish your business as a sole proprietorship. It is very important, for example, that you fully understand that as the sole owner or proprietor of the business, you are 100 percent responsible for everything that happens in the business. You cannot pass off responsibility to one of your employees on the grounds that you were not aware of what the employee was doing. You cannot walk away from any debts because you do not have the money to repay money owed. This concept is identified by lawyers as **unlimited liability**, meaning you have full responsibility for the activities of the business.

For example, as a sole proprietor, you are responsible for injuries suffered by customers and other visitors to your place of business if the injury suffered is the fault of your business. If, for instance, a business you own has a floor in need of repair and a customer's leg falls through the floor, resulting in serious injury, your individual assets could be at risk if the injured party wins a civil judgment for negligence against you as the sole proprietor.

Suppose, furthermore, that your sole proprietorship does not take in sufficient revenues to pay expenses, resulting in one of your suppliers not being paid. If this persists for a while, you may decide to close the business and declare bankruptcy. According to U.S. law, bankruptcy does not mean that you personally can walk away from the debt of a sole proprietorship. In fact, a sole proprietor is personally liable for any and all outstanding debts of the sole proprietorship even if the business closes its doors.

Similarly, if the business closes down and there are outstanding debts yet to be paid, you personally may be sued for repayment through a civil lawsuit against you as the owner. In this case, any remaining business assets (e.g., your store, office, warehouse, inventory, automobiles, computer devices, supplies) may be seized as well as your personal property (e.g., your home or car). In other words, **a sole proprietorship's debt is also your personal debt** if you are the owner of the business.

Another disadvantage to be aware of is that a sole proprietor assumes all the **risks** of running a business. There are no partners or board members sharing the risk. Business is not for people who are risk averse; businesspeople are by nature risk-takers who benefit during the good times and pay the price during bad times.

Also important to consider when establishing a sole proprietorship is **access to financial capital** to start and/or run your business. As the sole owner, for example, it may be difficult to secure external financing because only one owner is committing to repaying a loan secured from a bank. In this case, the banker will review your financial documents and determine how much money you are likely to be able to repay on your own. If you had a couple of partners, the banker might be more likely to offer a larger loan, confident that three people will have a better chance of repaying the loan rather than only one person.

One other disadvantage to note here is that when you establish a sole proprietorship, there is **no division of labor**. Running the business, at least initially, is a one-person show. You are the person to get up early and open the doors to your store and stay until the last customer leaves in the evening. You must order and track inventory. You must meet and work with customers. You are the bookkeeper and accountant. You are the chief salesperson and merchandiser. In other words, you are responsible for running all the functional areas of your business.

Depending on the industry you are in and the size of your endeavor, being a one-person show may suit your needs quite well. My noting some of the disadvantages is not to discourage you from starting your business as a sole proprietor, but rather to give you a heads-up on the things to be considered ex ante, that is, before you venture out on your own.

In sum, running a sole proprietorship can be extremely gratifying and lucrative as those of us who own businesses can attest. It can also be exhausting and trying at times. The trade-off between the advantages and disadvantages of owning and running a sole proprietorship can only be determined by you based on your unique business model, short- and long-term plans, and personality. Consult your most valued professors, mentors, and family members to help you sort through your options and inform your ultimate decision about setting up a business on your own.

Type 2: Partnerships

A second type of business structure in the United States is a partnership, enabling you to consider the possibility of going into business with other people. While some entrepreneurs strive to start and run their own enterprise, others go into business with the expressed desire to work with others who share a common goal, vision, and business interest, in which case a partnership may be worth considering.

Partnerships are **voluntary associations**, meaning each person engaged in the partnership must agree to work with the other partners. Just because you may be very close to possible partners, for example, siblings, it is unlawful for someone to list your name on a partnership agreement without your written consent. Hence, this emphasizes the voluntary nature of all business partnerships.

To form a partnership, at least two people must agree to work together. But the ultimate number of partners is up to you to decide. Remember that whoever you include in the partnership will be a co-owner of the business. If just two of you start the partnership, you split things two ways; if there are 15 partners, you split things 15 ways. While each partner is valued because they bring some resources to the business, it is important to remember that as the number of partners increases so does the time required for effective decision making, which may or may not be a detractor to your mind.

The key to choosing partners is the **pooling** of skills, knowledge, experience, contacts, money, time, energy, creativity, knowledge of the world, and anything else a potential partner may offer. Choose partners who will bring something that you cannot offer, hence building a strong group of diversified owners who can work together.

It is easy for us to think about creating a business partnership with people who are similar to us, such as people with whom we grew up, went to college, were members of the same sorority, frequent the same bar or church, played on a sports team, or share the same interests. While it is great to be able to work with people who have shared experiences, this may not be to your advantage from a business perspective. Perhaps, you could partner with people who have different life experiences, cultural backgrounds, and skills to diversify and strengthen your partnership.

In what industries do we tend to see partnerships? Most often, lawyers will establish their law practices as partnerships, identifying the key and/or founding partners in the name of the firm. Similarly, certified public accountants (CPAs), medical doctors, private equity firms, real estate agencies, and advertising agencies are likely to form businesses as partnerships. Because businesses owned by spouses do not qualify as sole proprietorships, family businesses are likely to be set up as partnerships.

Articles of Partnership

If you decide to establish your business as a partnership, the first step is to create a legal contract, known as the Articles of

Partnership. The document serves as an official agreement between all the partners regarding selected elements relevant to the business. Some of the key elements to include in a partnership agreement include the date the partnership commences, the names of the partners, the name of the business partnership you are establishing, the location of the business, the purpose of the partnership, a sunset clause articulating when and how the partnership will be terminated, the initial amount of cash each partner puts into the business, the salaries to be paid to each partner, and the share ratios each partner may claim from the profits (and losses).

It is up to you and your partners to determine these parameters. For example, even though each partner may initially contribute different sums of money to establish the business, you may determine that the profits and losses be shared equally. When calculating distribution shares, be sure to factor in the sum of all the resources, work, and know-how contributed to the business by each partner. While one person may have more money to initially invest in the business, another partner may have much more experience in this industry and time to invest in the day-to-day running of the business. There are trade-offs to be considered among the partners to establish terms that are acceptable.

Make an effort to specify as many potential differences between partners at the outset to avoid having difficulties in the event the partnership dissolves unexpectedly. I suggest a relatively short sunset clause in the event the partnership does not unfold as expected. If you have a clause that specifies that the duration of the partnership agreement be for 5 years, or for a shorter period if agreed upon by the partners, disbanding the partnership will be much less painful than if you have a 15-year sunset clause, which could prove untenable.

Once all the partners have agreed to the terms in the contract, the Articles of Partnership should be signed and dated by each partner.

Table 3.2 Statistics on partnerships

Number of Entities	4,500,186
Receipts (USD)	$12.5 trillion
Net Income (USD)	$2.6 trillion

Source: IRS. SOI Bulletin: Fall 2024.

Statistics on Partnerships

The IRS provides key data on partnerships in the United States in the quarterly IRS *SOI Bulletin*, as summarized in Table 3.2. These data reflect activities of all kinds of partnerships in the United States, including general partnerships, limited partnerships (LPs), joint ventures, and more.

The total number of partnerships registered in the United States as of 2024 was 4.5 million, 85 percent fewer than the 29.3 million registered sole proprietorships. Despite the smaller number of partnerships, the $12.5 trillion in annual receipts into partnerships was six-and-a-half times larger than receipts for sole proprietorships. How can this be? There are fewer partnerships, yet these partnerships bring in far more money than sole proprietorships.

Think back on our discussion of the types of industries where we tend to see businesses incorporated as partnerships: medical doctors, accountants, lawyers, and financial firms. All these professionals tend to charge relatively higher professional fees for services that are captured in the higher receipt figures. After everyone is paid, partnerships netted $2.6 trillion, significantly more than the $411 billion in net income for sole proprietorships.

Why Start Your Business as a Partnership?

Why do businesspeople set up their businesses as partnerships? What are some of the advantages compared to sole proprietorships? Like sole proprietorships, partnerships are easy to start.

One of the main considerations with a partnership is the time that must initially be devoted to seeking consensus among the partners as to what needs to be included in the all-important Articles of Partnership. There may be extra costs associated with consulting an attorney at law to be sure your contract meets the specific needs of your industry and partners.

Another advantage of a partnership is the ability to **pool resources** to establish, run, and grow your business. Think about what each partner could bring to your joint endeavor: prior experience in the industry or perhaps knowledge of one or more of the functional areas of business (e.g., finance, accounting, data science, supply-chain operations, advertising, public relations, and/or management). Partnerships also enable you to pool finances to get your business going.

In addition to pooling resources, partnerships are synonymous with **shared accountability**. No longer are you working on your own. You have partners with whom you may consult before making decisions. And no matter how things turn out, all of the partners have a stake in the outcomes.

One final benefit is that partnerships do not have to pay corporate income taxes because they are pass-through entities. Like sole proprietors, partners are allowed to report to the IRS their share of the business's income, expenses, profits, and losses directly on the personal income tax form (IRS Form 1040). This reporting mechanism will save the partners' time, effort, and money.

Downsides of General Partnerships

It is important to note that every one of the general partners in your business has 100 percent responsibility for what happens in the partnership. As we discussed when analyzing sole proprietorships, this concept is known as **unlimited liability**, meaning that everything related to the business is the responsibility of the individual partners. Articles of Partnership do not protect owners from personal liability for debts and harms caused by their business partnerships.

Unlimited liability is tricky in partnerships because it means that you are responsible for any business-related activities and decisions made by your partners, even if the partners did not inform you of their actions ahead of time. The lesson here is to know your partners well and only go into business with individuals who share your notion of honesty and ethical practices, because the actions of one partner have ramifications for all the other partners, definitely a downside of this form of business entity.

Also, the concept of unlimited liability differs somewhat in the case of LPs, discussed at the end of this chapter, whereby only one general partner holds unlimited liability, and the rest of the partners hold limited liability.

Valuable to note is that if a person has considerably more assets than the other potential partners, that person might consider the risks of becoming a partner. Under the law, a claimant may pursue a legal obligation such as a civil judgment against one partner or any number of partners. Therefore, it stands to reason that a person who wins a civil judgment against a partnership would pursue their financial award against the partner who has the deepest financial pockets.

To mitigate against surprises by your business partners, some people decide to open their partnerships with family members whom they know well. A case in point is the partnership established in 1963 by brothers Stanley and Sidney Goldstein, who opened a storefront that sold health and beauty products in Lowell, Massachusetts. The name of their business was **Con**sumer **V**alue **S**tores, which was later sold and became the nation's largest pharmacy—known simply as CVS—with a remarkable $358 billion in revenues in 2023.

Lastly, given that you are working side-by-side with other people who share ownership of this partnership, there may be **managerial disagreements** that can be arduous to handle. If you own your own business, you do not have to consult partners on how you might engage in the ongoing process of coordinating resources to reach your stated goals, the definition of management. Hence, management conforms to your style. Not so with partnerships, where it quickly becomes clear that owners may have different notions of how to oversee operations and make decisions.

Type 3: Corporations

In the United States, 2019 marked 200 years since a seminal moment occurred in the creation of a third type of business: the corporation.

In 1819, the U.S. Supreme Court handed down a ruling on an important case, *Trustees of Dartmouth College v. Woodward*, with the opinion written by Chief Justice John Marshall. As noted in the ruling, the Supreme Court gave extraordinary privileges to businesses holding private charters, allowing them to conduct business in a given state. Up to this point, private business charters were subject to state government oversight. But in 1819, the Supreme Court challenged state sovereignty over private corporate charters.

The Supreme Court did not regard the corporation as a type of citizen as was the case with sole proprietorships and partnerships, but rather as an *artificial entity* independent of the state. This legal case reflected the tensions in America at the time regarding what entity had the right to amend or repeal a corporate charter of a private commercial enterprise. The ruling deemed that corporate charters were not subject to changes by the state in which they were chartered, a ruling that was challenged for many decades yet prevailed and ultimately granted ever more autonomy to corporations.

How did the advent of this third type of business change commerce in the United States? The ruling established a new unit of analysis—the private corporation independent of state sovereignty—with rights that differed from sole proprietorships and partnerships. For example, a corporation could start a business and operate a business, as distinct from you (as an individual citizen) starting and operating a business. A corporation could buy and sell land, as distinct from individual citizens putting their names on land deeds. A corporation had the right to sue other entities (and persons) and be sued as well. A corporation could buy stock in another corporation. A corporation could enter into binding contracts.

All this may sound like no big deal. However, in the early 19th century, it was a big deal! The Supreme Court ruling fundamentally challenged the historical notion of business and determined that private corporate charters were "inviolate" and hence not subject to changes by state governments. It took some industrial magnates a long time to trust the new view on corporations, including steel magnate Andrew Carnegie, who consolidated his enormous business holdings into the Carnegie Steel Corporations in 1889 as a limited liability partnership to ensure his full control and ownership rights.

Over time, the notion of a third type of business, the private corporation, also known as a regular or C corporation, propelled the United States toward becoming a nation in which commerce was increasingly conducted by privately chartered corporations within our capitalist economic system.

Some of the most well-known businesses are corporations, primarily because of their size and scope. Financiers measure size in terms of a firm's market capitalization, calculated by multiplying the total number of shares traded on the stock market by the present share price.

As of June 2024, the largest corporations worldwide by market capitalization were the following:

1. Microsoft $3,151 billion
2. Nvidia $3,011 billion
3. Apple $3,003 billion
4. Alphabet $2,177 billion
5. Amazon $1,886 billion
6. Meta $1,255 billion
7. TSMC $845 billion
8. Broadcom $655 billion
9. Tesla $558 billion
10. Tencent $460 billion

Source: https://statistica.com.

Statistics on Corporations

Table 3.3 presents statistics on corporations, drawing from the IRS *SOI Bulletins* through tax year 2020 (the most recent year of available data). There are now more than 6.4 million corporations in the United States, far fewer than the 29.3 million sole proprietorships and only a bit more than the 4.5 million partnerships.

A different story emerges when we look at the dollars. The IRS reported that corporate receipts last count reached $33.4 trillion. This means that the dollar value of all receipts coming into corporations was larger than the entire $21 trillion U.S. economy in the same year. How much of these receipts did corporations keep? After all expenses were subtracted, corporations kept $2.7 trillion in net income, a sizable profit.

Table 3.3 Statistics on corporations

Number of Entities	6,402,130
Receipts (USD)	$33.4 trillion
Net Income (USD)	$2.7 trillion

Source: IRS. SOI Bulletin: 2020.

Why Start Your Business as a Corporation?

The establishment of the corporation as we know it enabled businesspeople to grow their enterprises in ways not possible through structures such as sole proprietorship or partnerships in a burgeoning global economy. What is it about corporations that distinguish them from other business types?

One factor is that corporations have access to more **financial capital** to establish and grow. For example, corporations have the right to sell stock in their firms as a means of raising equity capital. The idea of selling stock is to get other businesses, institutions, and individuals to give your business money in exchange for stock in the business.

Another key characteristic of the corporation is the notion that the owners do not have 100 percent responsibility for the activities of the business as is the case for sole proprietors and general partners who have unlimited liability. Rather, owners of a corporation and their representatives have what lawyers refer to as **limited liability**. In essence, corporations create a firewall between the owners and the corporation itself. If there is a problem with the business, the owners may not personally be sued in a civil lawsuit unless the owner has committed fraud in relation to business activities. By law, the corporation is treated as a legal person, separate from its founders, owners, the owner's representatives (e.g., executives and managers), and shareholders. Therefore, any aggrieved party must sue the corporation directly.

Similarly, if the business falls into debt, a creditor (or creditors) owed money must sue the corporation to make a claim on business assets instead of trying to secure payment through the owners' personal assets. Hence, corporate owners and their representatives are not at risk of losing their home or any other personal property in the event that a customer, creditor, or other agent is unhappy with what happens in the name of the corporation.

Another characteristic of a corporation is that the business will outlive the founders, owners, and their agents. The legal term is **perpetual life**. In contrast, if one of the co-owners in a general partnership dies, the business may or may not survive, depending on the terms specified in the Articles of Partnership.

Because corporations are endowed with the characteristics of personhood, another advantage of starting your business using this structure is the lawful ability of your corporation to lobby politicians and engage in electioneering; that is, the promotion of individual candidates for public office at the national, state, and municipal levels.

Downsides of Corporations

Starting a corporation is more difficult than starting either a partnership or sole proprietorship. Extra time and expense are required given the special laws and regulations pertaining to corporations. Hence, I recommend that if you decide to incorporate your business, consult an attorney to either handle such matters or help guide you through the process.

While corporations may remain small, most capitalize on the many advantages of the corporate form of organization to grow in size and scope over time, with its attendant challenges from a managerial perspective. In stark contrast to sole proprietorships, which can be run by one individual, it is rare that a corporation can be run by one person. Most corporations are staffed with employees who assume responsibility for each of the functional areas of business required to grow and be successful. Thus, the owners may not know all that is going on in a corporation, thus introducing challenges and problems that may be met with inflexibility due to size. In general, decision making takes longer in corporations compared to smaller entities.

Also viewed as a disadvantage when setting up your business as a corporation is the necessity to pay **corporate income taxes** on money earned, net of tax-deductible business expenses. C corporations must complete IRS Form 1120, the U.S. Corporation Income Tax Form, listing all income and expenditures. If the net income is non negative, the corporation must pay corporate income tax according to guidelines provided by the IRS.

Trends in Business Types

We conclude this chapter with some notes on trends in business structure, beginning with a comparative analysis across business structures and closing with an examination of special-purpose business types such as the LP, S corporation, Limited Liability Company (LLC), and Private Equity firms.

The IRS *SOI Bulletin* data allow us to create a picture of all the businesses in the United States today and contrast the relative sizes of sole proprietorships, partnerships, and corporations using data filings with the IRS to 2024.

The IRS reported that a total of 40.2 million businesses had the legal right to conduct business as corporations, partnerships, or sole proprietorships in the United States in 2024. To put that number in context, there is one business entity for every 8.2 people in the United States, which highlights the staggering amount of business activity in the country.

Out of these 40.2 million entities, a full 73 percent are sole proprietorships, underlining the general notion that small business is the backbone of America. Eleven percent of business entities are partnerships (of all kinds) and 16 percent are corporations.

With regard to business receipts as of 2024, the IRS reports that total receipts for all business entities were $48 trillion. Only 4 percent of receipts were earned by sole proprietorships, 26 percent by partnerships, and 70 percent by corporations, signifying the volume of business transactions occurring within private corporations.

Lastly, after all parties have been paid, including the IRS, $5.6 trillion remained as net income. Some 7 percent of net income went to sole proprietors, 45 percent to partnerships, and the remaining 48 percent to corporations.

Limited Partnership

Changes in statistical data provided by the IRS since the onset of the Great Recession in 2008 reveal that fewer businesspeople are setting up their enterprises as corporations. In contrast, the number of businesses registered as partnerships has risen, along with their receipts and net income earned.

Of particular interest is a rise in the formation of a particular kind of partnership known as a **Limited Partnership** since the beginning of the Wall Street financial crisis in 2007 and through the ensuing Great Recession. LPs are unique entities that in essence are a hybrid of the general partnership and the C corporation described earlier in this chapter.

Part Partnership: The LP hybrid leverages the unique advantages of partnerships and corporations to create a robust entity. LPs have the advantage of being smaller than most corporations, thus limiting the number of owners and providing a freer hand in managing the business. LPs are taxed like a partnership and hence pay no corporate income tax. LPs also have less public reporting, which saves time, energy, and money.

Part Corporation: At the same time, LPs are similar to corporations in that almost all of the business partners carry limited liability. By law, only one of the owners in an LP must hold unlimited liability and pay self-employment taxes toward Medicare and Social Security. The notion of perpetual life also applies to LPs, like corporations, and

LPs may raise money by issuing publicly tradable shares of stock, thus facilitating the securing of equity finance.

S Corporation

The other kind of corporation that exhibits traits of both partnerships and corporations is the **S corporation** under Subchapter 5 of the IRS code. The IRS established this kind of corporation post–World War II to encourage the creation of small Mom & Pop Shops. S corporations do not pay corporate income taxes; rather, owners report profits and losses on the IRS Form 1040 personal income tax form. All owners carry limited liability.

Constraints on S corporations include a limit of 100 allowable shareholders and a requirement that all shareholders be U.S. citizens or legal residents. Some states do not recognize the S corporation business structure and/or may put in place a cap on the total receipts such entities may earn, above which the business will be treated as a standard C corporation.

Limited Liability Company

Another type of corporation growing in popularity today is the **LLC**. In addition to members benefiting from personal limited liability protection, LLCs may choose how it will be taxed. If there are two or more partners, it may elect to be taxed like a partnership. If there is only one owner, it may be taxed as a sole proprietorship. The LLC has the option of being taxed as a regular C corporation or an S corporation.

The LLC is another example of a hybrid business entity emulating certain characteristics of corporations, partnerships, and sole proprietorships. LLC owners are called *members* who are protected against personal liability for all business activities, obligations, and debts. The members record profits and losses directly on their IRS Form 1040 as personal income that is not taxed as corporate earnings. Hence, financial activities pass through the LLC directly to the owner.

Of interest to the IRS is the recent use of the LLC business structure for philanthropic and lobbying activities. Some wealthy Americans are using the LLC private business structure to manage their philanthropic activities, including donations.

In the 20th century, wealthy businesspeople who gave away large portions of their wealth tended to establish private foundations. Per IRS guidelines, these entities are granted 501(c)(3) status as tax-exempt entities, meaning money donated to the private foundation could be deducted from the donor's personal income taxes. In return, private foundations are required to distribute at least 5 percent of the foundation's assets each year for charitable purposes, disclose the recipients of foundation grants, and not engage in lobbying or electioneering, according to the Tax Reform Act of 1969.

Meta founder, Mark Zuckerberg, opted to use the LLC mechanism to manage his and his wife's (Priscilla Chan) philanthropic endeavors. By funneling 99 percent of the couple's Facebook shares (valued at $45 billion) through an LLC, named the Chan Zuckerberg Initiative, Chan and Zuckerberg (a) retain control over how their money is invested or donated; (b) skirt the 5 percent private foundation mandatory payout requirements (which would require a $2.25 billion distribution each year on $45 billion of assets); (c) retain rights to lobby for political causes; (d) avoid public disclosure of what is done with the money in the LLC; and (e) may invest the money in their LLC not only in nonprofit entities but also for-profit business interests in the United States and abroad.

Zuckerberg and Chan joined the ranks of others who have channeled philanthropic ventures through an LLC. Zuckerberg's announcement on December 1, 2015, reflected a savvy business financial transaction based on keen knowledge of the legal factors governing business structures in the United States today, something every successful businessperson would benefit from understanding.

Private Equity Partnerships

Private equity firms have grown in size, complexity, and number in the 21st century. By 2024, they managed $12 trillion of assets globally and were worth more than $500 billion on the U.S. stock market (The Economist 2024). The largest four are Blackstone, Apollo, Carlyle, and KKR (i.e., Kohlberg, Kravis & Roberts). In 2023, there are more than 20,000 private equity and private-equity-backed companies in the United States, 50 percent more than five years ago.

Private equity has expanded its asset base to include hospitals, home health care, hospice care, dental offices, life insurers, retirement plans, residential property, motor-home sites, fast food restaurants, retailers, sports clubs, music catalogs, newspapers, veterinarian clinics, university endowments, banks, manufactures, public libraries, utilities, ethanol pipelines and other public infrastructure, physical therapy shops, corrections facilities, car rentals, and an array of other industries. For private equity, business is not about producing goods and services to sell to customers. Businesses are viewed as "bundles of assets to be bought, sold and endlessly manipulated for financial gain" (Levintova 2022, 18).

Private equity firms are established primarily to buyout companies on debt, engage in financial and operational engineering to boost the value of the acquired businesses, and ultimately spin them off and/or use the inflated assets as collateral for future investment gains for shareholders.

The two most common legal structures used in private equity deals are LPs and LLCs. Obviously, LPs are included in our statistics on partnerships. The IRS allows LLCs, however, to register as either partnerships or corporations. Since the start of the 21st century, businesspeople have increasingly opted to list LLCs as partnerships. By 2023, the IRS reported that 72 percent of all partnerships in the United States were LLCs (IRS, SOI Bulletin, Fall 2023).

Thus, with a growing number of private equity deals set up as partnerships, it is no wonder that the IRS is reporting rising net income from partnerships in the United States. This is certainly a phenomenon to watch.

Wrap Up

When starting a new business, do not be too concerned about choosing the type of structure to best meet your business vision. U.S. law is such that you may change your business type if needed over time, another reason we like to conduct business in the United States. However, knowing from the start the distinction between sole proprietorships, partnerships, and corporations will leave you with a better sense of the advantages and disadvantages of each type of legal structure.

CHAPTER 4

Growth Strategies

Thus far, we have defined what a business is, considered different types of business structures with an eye toward helping you select the legal framework that suits your interests, and considered how your business fits into the $28 trillion U.S. economy, with its business cycle fluctuations and 40 million enterprises competing with one another.

Next, we will explore ways that you can grow your business through the production of goods and services, another piece of our definition of business.

What Is a Business?
An organization
comprised of people
who produce goods and services
to sell
to earn a profit
distributed to stakeholders

For most businesses, the ultimate objective is to grow in size and scope to increase revenues and ultimately profits. Toward this aim, you have some choices to make. One avenue to pursue is finding ways to grow your business while staying in the United States, which is the focus of this chapter. Another avenue is to grow your business by going global, to be explored in the next chapter. We will examine both domestic and global avenues so that you come away with a full set of options to consider when the time is right.

While some students are eager to go global, others do not have the urge to travel and/or to run a business that requires engaging in commerce with businesspeople in other countries. There is no right or wrong here. As businesspeople, we think about our strengths as well as our weaknesses. The choice about growth strategies is yours. And if you decide to stay local, there are many ways that enable you to expand your business by doing what is familiar in your own country, discussed as follows.

Option 1: Domestic Growth From Within

Some businesspeople employ a strategy called *growth from within* to expand operations domestically. Imagine a scenario whereby you have started your own business, which is doing well. You have a loyal customer base, you produce products (or services) that are in demand, and you are making more in revenues than you expend in costs and, hence, are earning a profit. You are proud of your success and ready for more.

A *growth from within* strategy would entail doing more of what you already know works well for you and your customers. You might consider, for instance, producing a different type of product at an existing manufacturing facility. You might consider expanding your customer base by reaching out to a different age group. You might explore setting up a new production or sales base in a different location. In other words, continue what your business already does well but on a larger scale or scope.

The *growth from within* strategy has been used effectively at my university, Mount St. Mary's. Established in 1808 as Mount St. Mary's College, it is the second oldest Catholic institution of higher education in the United States, second to Georgetown University in Washington, DC. For more than a century and a half, the Mount educated young male students who were seeking baccalaureate and seminarian degrees.

In 1972, the Mount made a significant strategic decision to grow from within by allowing the all-male college to start admitting women. Overnight, the Mount's customer base doubled, a winning strategy, as almost 60 percent of the student body attending colleges in the United States today is female.

This strategy was met with ease from a logistical perspective given that the university had a history of offering degree programs on a beautiful campus with capable professors, staff, and administrators who delivered accredited baccalaureate programs. The Mount's core business model remained the same, with the only logistical difference being the need to build and operate a women's dormitory to accommodate the new female student body. This has been a successful decision by the Mount, whereby 62 percent of our most recent graduates were females.

Another growth spurt at the Mount began in 2006 when the Board of Trustees sought to elevate Mount St. Mary's College to university status, hence offering masters-level courses, programs, and degrees. With state approval in 2009, the institution was renamed Mount St. Mary's University and established the School of Business, School of Liberal Arts, School of Science and Mathematics, and School of Education, each of which offers graduate degrees. Today, more than 25 percent of Mount students are conducting graduate studies, another success story.

A second example of the growth from within strategy is Home Depot, the biggest U.S. hardware and home improvement chain and the third-largest bricks-and-mortar retailer, after Walmart and Costco (The Economist, 2024, 58). Founded in 1970, Home Depot's market value reached $350 billion by 2024, sales topped $150 billion, and operating margins were around 15 percent.

Home Depot attributes its success in part to an effective growth from within strategy, specifically expanding its clientele. Post-Covid-19 pandemic, the hardware store chain decided to focus less on do-it-yourself home repair shoppers and more on professional contractors and tradespeople in construction, landscaping, plumbing, roofing, swimming pools, and more.

This strategy has proven to be lucrative. Contractors tend to work on larger projects, purchase in greater quantities, and will pay to have Home Depot deliver materials directly to job sites. Home Depot also began piloting in 2022 an expanded financial program that offers tradespeople store credit as another way to solicit their business. In June 2024, Home Depot went a step further by purchasing the construction supply company, SRS Distribution Inc., from the private equity firm Leonard Green & Partners (LGP) for $18.25 billion. Home Depot is vertically integrating its supply chain to further ensure that the iconic orange apron retailer remains competitive.

Option 2: Domestic Licensing

While there are many advantages to starting and running your business as a sole proprietor, you will quickly find that there is a limit to how much money you can earn.

If you own a CPA firm, for example, there is a cap on your billable hours each week. The same holds true for teachers, researchers, excavators, carpenters, lawyers, physical therapists, or plumbers established as sole proprietorships, whose earnings are constrained not by skill or knowledge but by time.

One way that you can grow your business while retaining sole ownership is through licensing your business model to capable service providers interested in what you do for a living. This is a very popular model among yoga teachers today. After years of training as yogis and running their own studios, yoga teachers are growing their businesses by setting up trademarked yoga-teaching training schools that grant students the right to teach yoga under a proprietary brand name or trademark.

This is a form of licensing whereby the yoga teacher (and business owner) works with people who want to become licensed yoga instructors. The owner shares her knowledge and experience accumulated running a yoga studio. The students pay to train with the yogi for a set number of contact hours (200, 300, 500), after which the student receives a diploma, indicating she is fit to teach yoga. Some yogi business owners go one step further and franchise their yoga studios to students who have gone through the owner's formal yoga teacher training programs.

The trick with this model, however, is to include a noncompete agreement that limits your students' ability to set up yoga studios in the vicinity of your studio. Geographic noncompete clauses date back to the guilds in 15th- and 16th-century Europe, where young apprentices were barred from opening a shop in the same town as their mentors to avoid the possibility of stealing customers. This is where the term *journeymen* first appeared, meaning once you received your training, you had to journey down the road so you could not compete with your mentor.

PLANK

Option 3: Domestic Mergers and Acquisitions

Another example of how to grow your business domestically is via a merger and acquisition (M&A) with a firm in the same country in which you operate.

Mergers and acquisitions, commonly referred to as M&As, enable businesses to consolidate operations to grow. Mergers are usually voluntary consolidations between two businesses eager to become one new entity, such as when the oil giant Exxon paid $79 billion to purchase Mobil Oil in 1998 and became ExxonMobil.

An acquisition may be a targeted and/or hostile takeover of one business by another with the intention of doing away with the competition and dominating an industry. An example was Elon Musk's hostile takeover of Twitter in 2022 for $44 billion. If both business entities involved in the M&A are registered to do business in the same country, this is considered a domestic growth strategy.

The number and type of M&As has changed over time. Historically, the United States experienced M&A peaks during the 1890s, 1920s, 1960s, late 1980s, 1990s, and mid-2010s. Various precipitating events trigger M&A activities, for example, economic shocks like the explosive growth in personal computers in the 1990s and artificial intelligence (AI) in the 2020s. Mergers also may be the result of a quick drop in aggregate demand among buyers in an industry, leaving excess capacity ripe for acquisition. Significant changes in the regulatory environment may also lead to mergers, as well as changes in financial conditions such as the buildup of large amounts of cash on the balance sheets of digital platform firms beginning in the mid-2010s that led to the buyout of many smaller digital firms that held the promise of becoming serious competitors to dominant firms.

One of the largest domestic M&As transpired in 2023 when Microsoft acquired Activism Blizzard for $75.4 billion. Activision Blizzard sells some of the most popular egames, including Call of Duty, Overwatch, World of Warcraft, and Candy Crush.

Microsoft was eager to get into the gaming industry for several key reasons. First, gaming is one of the largest entertainment industries in the world. Statista estimated that worldwide gaming revenues topped $347 billion in 2022, of which mobile gaming generated $248 billion (https://statista.com).

Second, videogaming consoles (e.g., Sony's PlayStation, Sega, Nintendo, and MS's Xbox) are being replaced with cloud-based paid subscription services, allowing gamers to play anywhere and anytime. Microsoft's Azure is the second largest cloud platform and is building its library of popular games, which now includes the Activism Blizzard games, a boon for Microsoft.

Third, Microsoft was willing to buyout Activision Blizzard knowing that each person who plays egames generates troves of data that a digital platform could mine and monetize. Online gaming harvests data about individuals and communities alike. Players reveal, for example, information on their finances, the way they use money, their social lives, artistic and creative preferences, and other interactive user activities. Such data collection feeds into Microsoft's algorithms and operations, which in turn advances their competitiveness in the gaming industry (see Kokas 2023).

A fourth reason behind the acquisition is knowing that the data collected from global egamers can be used to feed Microsoft's AI models, the future of the cloud computing industry, discussed in Chapter 10.

Types of M&As

From a business perspective, a merger or acquisition is a form of investment. There are three major kinds of M&As, each of which serves a unique business purpose.

Horizontal M&As entail the purchase of one business by another business engaged in the same industry or line of operation, for example, one shoe manufacturer buying another shoe manufacturer. The result of horizontal integration is to limit the competition within a particular industry.

Cellular carriers made the news between 2017 and 2022 with talk of a possible merger between the Sprint Corporation (valued at $33 billion in 2017) and T-Mobile US Inc. (valued at $41 billion). When measured by the number of mobile subscribers, Sprint was the third-largest carrier in the United States, followed by T-Mobile. Combining operations would result in a single carrier with 126 million subscribers. Merger talks were of great interest to competitors Verizon Wireless and AT&T.

In 2022, T-Mobile US successfully acquired the Sprint Corporation for $26 billion. The aim was to create a firm with the potential to dominate 5G wireless communication in the United States. The merger bumped T-Mobile's standing in the wireless industry. By the fourth quarter of 2022, 39 percent of wireless subscribers used Verizon, 31 percent used T-Mobile (including Sprint), and 30 percent used AT&T.

In an effort to upscale its image, Walmart has also aggressively engaged in horizontal M&As by purchasing the small niche online clothing boutique Bonobos in 2017 for $310 million. The year prior, Walmart purchased ShoeBuy, Moosejaw.com, ModCloth.com, and Jet.com, signaling an effort to move beyond a no-frills image, attract more affluent urban online shoppers, and push up its prices. Horizontal M&As may help Walmart expand its customer base in the increasingly competitive retail industry that is challenging Walmart's status as the world's largest retailer.

Walmart

In contrast to a horizontal merger, a **vertical M&A** entails a firm buying a business that is part of its supply chain rather than a direct competitor. The objective is for the acquiring business to exercise more control over its supply chain in the hopes of increasing profits.

Walmart is just as skillful in vertical M&As as horizontal M&As. In 2022, Walmart bought out two firms that were in their supply chain. The first was Symbotic, a robotics and software automation firm. The second was Volt Systems that tracks customer data. Both acquisitions reflect Walmart's aim to expand its capacity to collect, analyze, and profit from data collection.

A much-talked-about vertical merger that was negotiated in 2017 and 2018 was between the oldest health insurer in the country, Aetna ($63 billion in revenues), and the largest U.S. pharmacy, CVS Health ($177 billion in revenues). CVS Health successfully acquired Aetna in 2018 for $70 billion. The M&A sought to bring together three key layers of the health industry supply chain:

- Retail pharmacies (that fill prescriptions)
- Pharmacy benefits managers and intermediaries (that negotiate drug prices for medical plans)
- Health-care insurers

The U.S. DOJ approved the CVS Health and Aetna $70 billion merger on October 10, 2018. CVS moved aggressively to seek approval of the buyout to drive Aetna's 22 million health insurance enrollees to CVS Health's 9,700 pharmacies and 1,000 Minute Clinics.

The urgency of the offer was fueled by speculation that ecommerce giant Amazon.com Inc. would soon acquire more pharmacies, build pharmacies into its Whole Foods Market grocery stores, and expand its mail order and delivery prescription drug model.

Because the U.S. DOJ concerns itself primarily with horizontal mergers when enforcing antitrust laws, it approved the CVS–Aetna merger, which it viewed as a vertical M&A rather than a horizontal M&A. The CVS–Aetna deal might well become a template for other vertical mergers in not only the health industry but also other industries.

Vertical M&As have an historical precedent in the United States, dating back to the captains of industry during the Gilded Age (late 1870s to 1900). John D. Rockefeller, for example, set up Standard Oil as a vertically integrated business by acquiring as many elements as he could in the oil supply chain, from land and oil wells to refineries and delivery wagons. Henry Ford did the same when founding the Ford Motor Company on the belief that "If you want it done right, do it yourself" (Ford 1926).

Despite the long-term success of vertical integration, U.S. businesses steered away from this model in the 1980s in favor of subcontracting out pieces of their supply chains to reduce costs and retain only core business elements.

Forty years later, firms are returning to the practices of the turn-of-the-20th-century industrialists, arguing that doing things in-house is more efficient and quicker than contracting out pieces of the supply chain. Thus, we see Netflix and Amazon creating their own content for television shows and movies viewed by customers who might otherwise seek content from competitors on cable, network television, and/or other streaming services. The benefits of vertical integration propelled Costa Cruises and Walt Disney to purchase Caribbean islands to ensure a pleasant experience for sea-faring customers and avoid geopolitical uncertainties impacting their growing businesses.

In addition to vertical and horizontal M&As, there are **conglomerate M&As**, whereby the parties involved in negotiations are neither direct competitors nor part of each other's supply chain. Rather than specialize in a single industry (e.g., banking, automobiles, retail trade, steel, and software), businesses are branching out to establish themselves as conglomerates that reach across an array of industries, products, and services.

The formation of conglomerates was a popular strategy in the 20th century, when internationally minded corporations vastly diversified portfolios by purchasing nonrelated businesses with the aim of rapid growth and expansion across the globe. Such was the case when Andrew Carnegie sold his famed Carnegie Steel Company to financier J.P. Morgan in 1901, reflecting the banker's diversified portfolio strategy. On July 8, 1986, J.P. Morgan renamed its U.S. Steel division to simply U.S.X. to reflect the firm's further diversification well beyond steel.

The historical roots in diversification through conglomerate M&As appears to be back in vogue in the 21st century. Growing interest in conglomerates is now a global phenomenon.

Amazon.com Inc. provides a visible, large-scale illustration of a conglomerate in the United States today, as envisioned by founder Jeff Bezos. Established in 1996 as an online bookstore, Amazon grew into an empire that includes physical bookstores, online retail sales of all types of goods and services, drone manufacturers, autonomous humanoid robotic research, military contracting, newspapers, sports media, organic retail grocery stores, and generative AI applications.

Bezos's growth strategy experiments have been remarkably successful: 56 percent of all consumers start their online shopping purchases on Amazon.com, and 38 percent of all ecommerce sales go to Amazon. With total revenues in 2023 topping $575 billion, Amazon relentlessly strives to expand its scope and reach.

amazon.com

Parallel Entrepreneurs

In frontier economies, where there is rapid growth and a burgeoning consumer middle class, we are seeing a spin-off of conglomerates, referred to as *parallel entrepreneurs*, emerging. Parallel entrepreneurship refers to businesspeople who create, own, and run a network of different business entities across an array of industries within one country. These entities are neither conglomerates run by one firm nor are they set up to be potentially merged with or acquired by another business. Rather, the owner sees a benefit in owning several distinct legal entities engaged in different activities.

Africa is a case in point. Why? Some entrepreneurs are capitalizing on the wealth of business opportunities in countries such as Ghana, Nigeria, and Kenya, where entrepreneurs own, on average, six businesses each. Parallel entrepreneurs report that once they have established a high level of trust among customers, it is easy to introduce another service to the same customers, especially in businesses that are relationship-based (e.g., management consulting, finance, and internet service providers [ISPs]).

Parallel entrepreneurs also indicate that at times it may be easier to raise small amounts of money for each business rather than raise a large sum for a single entity. In addition, African businesspeople often face unpredictability vis-à-vis national policies, laws, and government officials that deters them from putting all their money into a single business. In these cases, a diversified set of business interests may be advantageous.

The venerable Tata family business, founded in 1868 in India by Jamshedji Tata, known as the **Tata Group**, represents one of the largest parallel entrepreneurships in the world, with 100 divisions and 29 publicly listed enterprises in 2023. The family business strategy extended operations well beyond its key revenue-makers in steel, motor vehicles, power, telecoms, information technology (IT), and hotels to now include salt, Tata Global Beverages, chemicals, transportation, Tata Consulting Services, Tata Asset Management, Tata Management and Training Centre, Taj Hotels Resorts and Palaces, defense, infrastructure, and finance.

From 1868 to 2012, the Tata Group was overseen by a member of the Tata family. The last Tata boss was the world-renowned Ratan Tata, who oversaw an increase in his family firm's revenues from $6 billion to $100 billion between 1991 and 2012 with a global workforce of about 700,000 people in over 80 countries. Tata is now India's largest parallel entrepreneurship, with a combined market value of $300 billion (2023) and operations in 100 countries.

Tata represents a new kind of highly diversified, global transnational corporate enterprise on the rise in frontier economies across the globe, challenging traditional Western business structures and growth strategies.

Option 4: Breaking Up a Business

One other way to grow your business is quite the opposite of a merger and acquisition. It is possible for a firm to realize that, in an effort to grow, it may be advantageous to break up the firm into separate businesses. Such was the case in 2018 when Larry Culp, CEO of General Electric (GE), indicated that the conglomerate was considering selling divisions worth $20 billion (out of $365 billion in total assets) and restructuring GE into three core operations: GE Aviation, GE Health, and energy-based GE Vernova.

This sell-off is an attempt to rid GE of nonperforming assets, to reverse its share price decline, and position each of the three new units to succeed globally. Culp was also well-aware of the implications of the Dow Jones Industrial Average's removal of GE from its 30-firm index in June 2018, despite GE having been one of the Dow's original components in 1896. On April 2, 2024, the venerated conglomerate ceased to exist when it spun off into three publicly traded enterprises, which GE refers to as its "go forward" companies (www.ge.com/).

Wrap Up

Whether you are in a highly competitive industry or one with little competition, there are a host of ways that you can grow your business in addition to the options presented in this chapter. Read on to explore further growth options by going global.

CHAPTER 5

Going Global

Today, studying business is unlike anything we have seen before. In the past, business schools would differentiate between the study of business and the study of global business. Today, they are one and the same in many ways.

When studying M&As, for example, we can apply what we learn to businesses in any country around the world. If we study finance, we can apply our new knowledge to global arbitrage and finance across the globe. If we determine that marketing and public relations is our favorite functional area, we can use our new tools in any location.

Our world is incredibly intertwined. There are 195 countries on planet Earth, of which 193 are member states of the United Nations, with the remaining two being nonmember observer states: the Vatican and the State of Palestine. Politicians and diplomats work diligently to engage with businesspeople the world over in dynamic ways. Cultures vary incredibly from country to country. Languages are rich and varied throughout the world, where some 7,000 languages are spoken. Electronics and digitization enable us to communicate globally every day, 24 hours a day. Global business supply chains have become even more expansive as there are fewer barriers to interconnectedness. Jobs in business can take us anywhere on the planet, as my career demonstrates, and I hope yours will too.

It is a very exciting time to study business—global business—because global capitalism reaches almost every corner of our planet in the 21st century. It is fascinating to figure out how your business might be able to expand globally or at least connect with businesses, financiers, and consumers in other countries. Thanks to global capitalism, this is all very real and possible for you today.

Global Capitalism

What do I mean when using the term *global capitalism*? In a nutshell, global capitalism encapsulates the following:

> *Global capitalism is an economic framework to understand how society chooses to organize itself to meet economic, social, and financial needs.*

> *Global capitalism promotes competition in one single world economy.*

> *Global capitalism enables material, human, and financial resources to flow freely around planet earth.*

> *Global capitalism creates a structure and process by which businesses can expand across the planet.*

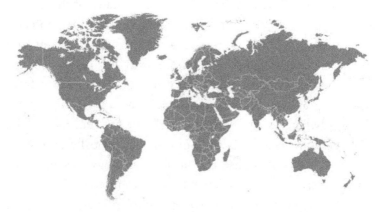

To paint a picture of global capitalism, consider salient statistics from 2023 that capture the imagination and boggle the mind:

- Transnational trade flows were valued at $24 trillion.
- Global gross domestic product (GDP) was estimated to be $105 trillion.

- About 184 million international migrants work worldwide.
- Official foreign exchange reserves total $12 trillion.
- $5 trillion in electronic currencies moves around the planet daily.

I am fascinated with the phenomenon called global capitalism that is sweeping the globe in full view and have made it my life's work to understand its nuances and how it impacts us from a business perspective. Perhaps, you will do the same.

Terminology

Our exploration into the world of business today can get complicated fairly quickly. Hence, our terminology has evolved. In the last two decades of the 20th century, any reference to commerce outside the United States was called **international** business, building on the simple two-country trade model introduced by neoclassical economists in the 19th century. By the end of the 20th century, global business had expanded well beyond the two-country trade model and required new terminology. Businesspeople settled on the term *multinational* to represent two or more nations conducting business together. Later, with finance, global arbitrage, big data, and global supply chains leading us toward a whole new understanding of global commerce, we often speak of **transnational** corporations (TNCs).

TNCs exhibit the following characteristics:

1. TNCs are corporate legal entities as defined by respective governments.
2. TNCs conduct business across borders, whereby two or more nations are engaged.
3. TNCs tend to be large business entities.
4. TNCs have no allegiance to any one country (or locality).

Think about how the world-renowned TNC **Disney Entertainment** produces its iconic films under global capitalism. The movie concept might be conceived in country A; the writers are in country B; the animation is created in country C; filming takes place in countries D and E; Disney buys parts and supplies for filming from countries A, B, and C; the final product is sent to fulfillment centers in country G, and it is ultimately sold to viewers in countries A through Z.

As we enter the second quarter of the 21st century, further wordsmithing seems apropos. Instead of referring to the largest businesses as transnational, might we refer to them as *transcontinental* corporations?

How You Can Go Global With Your Business

If you are ready to consider going global with your business, what are some of your options? Following are seven options to get you thinking. While not all-inclusive, perhaps when you are ready, you'll refer back to this list for ideas.

Option #1: Global Licensing

Suppose you own and run a manufacturing plant located in the United States that produces a line of clothing and accessories for sale domestically. For years you have wanted to expand your handbag line and have had your eye on **Louis Vuitton** products. What are your options? One idea is to approach Louis Vuitton in France and explore the possibility of establishing a business-to-business global licensing agreement.

Louis Vuitton is a world-renowned maker of purses, handbags, wallets, shoes, clothing, and luggage that dates back to 1854 when a man named Louis Vuitton started the business. Since his death, the firm has continued to grow and expand its product line and is part of the mega corporation LVMH (Moët Hennessy Louis Vuitton) run by the French founder, chair and

CEO Bernard Arnault (the third richest person in the world). The firm may be interested in granting you a license to use its manufacturing techniques to produce Louis Vuitton handbags in your U.S.-based manufacturing plant in return for a licensing fee.

Global licensing agreements are possible in an array of industries. In exchange for a licensing fee, the grantor of the license will provide what is needed for the foreign business to legally reproduce its products (e.g., recipes, patents, training). The Louis Vuitton purses you manufacture and sell would be sold as originals, with a sensor inside to verify its authenticity, and bear a label that says, "Made in the USA." Most consumers would have no clue that your business is engaged in global commerce.

Global licensing allows you to take your business global without your having to leave the United States, which is an advantage for some businesspeople.

Option #2: Foreign Direct Investment

One of the downsides of Louis Vuitton granting global licensing agreements is the risk that the business that pays for a license does not reproduce the handbags according to Louis Vuitton's strict quality standards. If this persists, Louis Vuitton risks having its reputation impugned. So, let's consider a second option to go global to mitigate such risk.

Option #2 is what is known as foreign direct investment (FDI). In this case, for example, a U.S. business might consider investing in a business in another country that has a strong business model and potential for expansion. The U.S. firm does not buy out the entire business but rather makes an equity investment by buying a stake of at least 10 percent in the foreign business.

Conversely, a foreign business might be interested in investing money in a U.S. business through the FDI vehicle. This kind of equity investing goes on all around the world and is tracked each year by the United Nations. In 2023, total FDI was estimated to be $1.33 trillion, down 2 percent from 2022. The United Nations' *World Investment Report* shows in detail how FDI changes from year to year and lays out which countries are doing the investing and which countries receive the most money (2024). In 2023, the largest source of FDI was the United States, followed by Japan and China. The largest FDI recipients were the United States, China, and Singapore.

FDI is what is known as an equity mode of investing directly in another business. In contrast, a licensing agreement is a non-equity mode of going global. Both options allow you to go global without leaving the United States.

Option #3: Global Mergers and Acquisitions

Like domestic M&As, global M&As present a mechanism for businesses to work together cross-border, voluntarily or involuntarily. Usually, mergers are voluntary associations between the owners and agents of two businesses that would mutually benefit by becoming a single business entity. Involuntary associations, in contrast, are not necessarily an advantage for both parties. The asymmetry stems from one business taking over another by becoming the majority shareholder or dominant voice on the board of directors.

Let's look at some recent M&As that involve businesses registered in two different countries.

S&P Global is a data analytics firm and rating agency with 100,000 customers in 150 countries. It is headquartered in New York City. In November 2020, S&P Global announced that it was interested in buying London-based IHS Markit, also a data provider that supplies financial information, market intelligence, and credit ratings to 50,000 customers in business and government. S&P Global offered to pay $44 billion for IHS Markit to create a one-stop-shopping service for clients.

Douglas Peterson, President and CEO of S&P Global said that the aim of the merger was to boost the combined firm's expertise in AI, machine learning services, and risk management, increasingly valuable to the financial information services industry.

The merger was completed on February 28, 2022. IHS Markit is now a wholly owned subsidiary of S&P Global in New York.

Verizon Wireless

One of the largest global M&As was between Verizon Communications and Vodafone, both of whom owned part of Verizon Wireless (established 1999).

When merger talks began in 2013, Verizon Wireless was the largest mobile service carrier in the United States. Verizon Communications, registered in the United States, owned 55 percent, and Vodafone, registered in England, owned 45 percent. With the aim of complete ownership and control of Verizon Wireless, on September 2, 2013, Verizon Communications announced a friendly buyout of all of Vodafone shares for $130 billion.

The Verizon Wireless buyout was the third largest business transaction in recorded history, preceded by the Vodafone Airtouch $198 billion takeover of Germany's Mannesmann and the AOL/Time Warner $165 billion merger, which both took place in 2000. The sheer size of these three M&As attests to the importance of the wireless communication industry then and now.

Option #4: Global Manufacturing

Industries engaged in manufacturing products may also go global to grow the business. Take, for example, a factory located in the United States that produces automobiles.

If you wanted to take this business global, there are a couple of possibilities to consider. First, you would review where the inputs to producing the cars in your factory come from. It is possible that all the materials required to assemble a car are made in the United States, for example, steel, tires, aluminum, leather, nuts and bolts, computer chips, and so on. If you have connections with suppliers of these inputs and are happy with their products, you may have no incentive to look elsewhere for suppliers. But if you want to consider other sources that may produce a better or a cheaper product, then global manufacturing may be preferable. In this case, you would travel the world interviewing businesses in foreign countries that produce the specific inputs needed for production. If an agreement is made, you would then import these products into the United States and transport them to your factory.

A second way to go global if you are a manufacturer is on the back end; meaning, after you have purchased all the necessary inputs to production and assembled the car, you may opt to sell not only to dealerships in the United States but also to dealerships in other countries. In this case, exporting the finished product is a way to go global and grow your business.

Option #5: Big Box Store

Another option to go global is the Big Box Store model, a phenomenon that swept the world due to the remarkable capabilities of logistics firms. Modern-day shipping and other transportation systems have enabled consumers to purchase goods manufactured across the planet at an affordable price. Commerce in the United States changed dramatically over the past century from being a system primarily driven by small entrepreneurs who owned and operated sole proprietorships catering to a local clientele. Today, transcontinental corporations dominate commerce and have created a system whereby place matters less and less.

Consider, for example, the creation of the world's largest retail chain, Walmart, started by Sam Walton in 1962, when he opened the first Walmart Discount City story in Rogers, Arkansas. His one-stop business model set the stage for a host of followers such as Target, Costco, Lowes, and more.

In contrast to global manufacturers described in Option #4, big box stores do not produce any of the products sold in their retail stores. Rather, the stores comb the globe for cheap producers of the products the operators think will sell in their locale and then import these products. In this case, big box stores are nonasset corporations, meaning they do not own the factories that produce the items sold in their stores.

While the model is simple, getting things from foreign countries into the United States is not simple. The U.S. Department of Homeland Security and the Bureau of Customs and Border Protection must approve and screen every item that enters the country. Any business engaged in importing products to be sold in their stores must have in-house expertise about how these agencies operate to adhere to the policies and procedures associated with importation.

For example, items that are imported into the United States may be subject to an import tax, known as a **tariff**. We are all familiar with the concept of taxes, as each time we purchase an item in a big box store, we must pay a consumption tax that varies from state to state. The U.S. International Trade Commission in Washington, DC, presents a detailed list each year of specific tariffs that must be paid when importing items into the United States for commercial purposes, called the Official Harmonized Tariffs Schedule. Thousands of tariffs are included in the listing.

There are two standard types of import duties, or tariffs. The first is a specific U.S. dollar amount that must be paid for each item imported. Each wristwatch your business imports, for example, would incur a 51¢ import duty. The second type of tariff is an ad valorem tax, which is a percentage of the worth of the product being imported (i.e., total cost of the product plus freight and insurance). While each watch you import costs you 51¢, a case or strap for a watch is charged an ad valorem tax of 6.25 percent and a watch battery 5.3 percent. For 2024, the U.S. International Trade Commission reports that the average tariff was 2 percent on merchandise imports.

Becoming a specialist in import tariffs is a great career path that enables you to work with a host of businesses engaged in imports and exports. You will also become familiar with the vast array of products produced, exported, and imported each year, which continues to grow in size and scope.

Option #6: Overseas Operations

As we move forward with further options for you to go global with your business, you will see that the level of complexity expands. We began with going global options that enabled you to continue to live and work in the United States (e.g., global licensing and foreign direct investing) and then progressively added layers of complexity (e.g., global M&As, global manufacturing, and big box stores).

Option #6 is even more interesting by virtue of it being the most global in terms of physical operations. Take the example of a U.S.-based factory that has successfully demonstrated its ability to produce products to sell to a loyal customer base in return for positive profits distributed to the stakeholders. Based on such success, your business may decide to consider moving its entire factory to another country.

This is a big decision that would engage your business in new and exciting ways. You would need, for example, to decide what country to consider and whether you want to rent space for your manufacturing facility or lease land on which to build a new facility. You would need to hire someone familiar with human resource policies and practices in the host country. You would need to establish relationships with new bankers. You would need to consult your existing employees to see who might be interested in moving to another country. The list goes on.

But if you do decide to move your entire operations overseas, your engagement with global commerce expands. For example, you would need to rethink where to secure the inputs for production in the overseas factory. Indeed, you could choose to keep using your loyal U.S.-based suppliers, some of whom may have supplied your business with inputs for many years. In this case, you would need to explore the costs associated with shipping and importing those supplies into the new country. Another possibility, not exclusive of the first, is to find some suppliers who are closer to where you now operate. This could include suppliers in the host country as well as suppliers in neighboring countries.

Once you have successfully started up your new overseas factory and are producing products, your next task is to think about customers. Hopefully, you will find a way to continue to sell to your loyal customers who have come to rely upon your products. In this case, you will incur the added costs of exporting your products from the new plant back to the United States. In addition, you might explore the option of developing a new customer base in the host foreign country.

While the previous example pertains to a manufacturing facility, the notion of overseas operations applies equally to the service industries. All the major U.S. banks, for example, have successfully established overseas operations to provide financial services to a global customer base (e.g., Citigroup, JP Morgan Chase, Bank of America, and Wells Fargo).

In the 2020s, firms began experimenting with "global capability centers" (GCCs) to offshore tasks to other countries. India is a case in point. The global capability centers in the Embassy Manyata Business Park in Bangalore and elsewhere in India are home to Lululemon, Maersk, Samsung, Wells Fargo, Nvidia, Intel, Boeing, Walmart, Mercedes-Benz, and other firms that hire well-educated, white collar workers to perform tasks such as research and development (R&D), data analysis, cloud computing, design work, and videoconferencing. The number of GCCs in India rose from 700 in 2010 to 1,580 in 2024 and employ some 3.2 million workers (NASSCOM, 2024).

Just as U.S. businesses have engaged in overseas operations, so have foreign businesses set up operations in the United States. One such firm is Lidl, a German discount grocery chain. In 2017, Lidl opened nine stores in Virginia, North Carolina, and South Carolina. By mid-2024, there were 175 Lidl stores in the United States, a figure that caught the attention of U.S. retailers Kroger and Walmart.

Lidl (est. 1973) is following the lead of their German rival, Aldi (est. 1961), which has opened more than 2,300 stores in 39 states and territories since 1976. The customer base of both firms is low- and middle-class shoppers seeking deep discounts on groceries. One of the key differences between the German Lidl and Aldi grocery store model and their U.S. competitors is that the German stores sell about one-tenth the number of items. The German stores are also privately held, offering more decision-making flexibility for managers than their larger publicly traded competitors.

Option #7: Global Franchising

We'll end our going global options with global franchising, which is similar to the global licensing option we started with, only with a twist. Franchising is a form of business-to-business licensing; however, I believe it warrants examination as a separate option because it is a unique and popular form of licensing and an option you might consider if you want to start and run your own business.

Every year, Franchise Direct, a national franchise association in the United States, releases a *Top 100 Global Franchises* list. The rankings reflect a host of variables, such as the number of franchise units, revenues, stability and growth, number of years in operation, and expansion.

Let's compare and contrast the top 10 global franchises in 2019 (pre-Covid pandemic) and 2024 (most recent data).

2019

1. McDonald's
2. Burger King
3. Pizza Hut
4. Marriott International
5. KFC
6. Dunkin'

7. 7-Eleven
8. Subway
9. Domino's
10. Baskin-Robbins

2024

1. The UPS Store
2. Budget Blinds
3. Kitchen Tune-Up
4. Ace Handyman Services
5. Anago Cleaning Systems
6. Five Star Bath Solutions
7. PuroClean
8. Visiting Angels
9. AAMCO
10. Griswold Home Care

What changes do you notice immediately between the top global franchisors in 2019 and 2024? First, in 2019, the list was dominated by fast food and hotels. Before the global pandemic, people ate out a lot and traveled for vacation and work. By 2024, none of the top franchisors were in the food or hotel industries. Second, in 2024, the list was dominated by home services, including renovations and cleaning. In a postpandemic world, people are more focused on their homes, which might also serve as a place of work.

How does a global franchise work? It starts with a business owner, called the *franchisor*, who might own a chain of restaurants in the United States but wants to expand globally. One possibility is for the owner to go to a foreign country and set up overseas operations, as we discussed in Option #6. This would be going global; however, it would be difficult for the owner to be in more than one place at a time. So, the person may decide to sell a franchise license to a *franchisee* in a foreign country.

The franchisee pays a license fee to the franchisor plus franchising royalties as determined and agreed upon between the two parties. In return, the franchisee in the foreign country receives help from the franchisor to set up and successfully run operations. Such assistance could include training on how to lay out and run the store, marketing by the franchisor, public relations assistance, a trademark, the brand name use, management skills, special recipes, and access to suppliers used by the franchisor.

If you are ready to start your own business but do not have a specific business idea, you might consider running your own franchise business and benefit from all that the franchisor can offer to get you on your way. In return for all the assistance provided by the franchisor, the franchisee agrees to abide by the provisions of the franchise agreement and the franchisee provides the labor and capital to run the business. The franchisee operates the franchise business as a sole proprietorship.

Wrap Up

The abovementioned ideas for going global are by no means exhaustive as there are many other options or a combination of options to consider. This list, however, gives you a sense of what it means to go global with your business interests and a place to begin when you are ready.

CHAPTER 6

Entrepreneurship

In this chapter, we explore another *functional area of business*, namely entrepreneurship and small business development. This takes us on a journey of discovering new ideas and possible ways to bring those ideas to fruition in the form of a new business entity, a new service or product, and/or a new business model that makes money.

Generating Ideas

Many businesses begin with a novel idea. When coupled with the drive to get an idea out to the public, these ideas can lead to success stories. How do businesspeople come up with ideas? Is everyone successful? What are some of the key factors to consider to be a successful entrepreneur? What are the possible risks associated with setting up your own business?

When asked, all entrepreneurs have stories to share as to the inception of the idea that resulted in their successful businesses. For some, the key was being a keen observer of people, society, and human behavior.

They figured out what would capture peoples' interest at a particular time in history. They were curious to learn which products people no longer purchase and which ones people are likely to continue purchasing. They discovered what other entrepreneurs did to turn ideas into thriving enterprises. They learned, through acute observation and study, what ideas failed and why.

Other entrepreneurs report that their ideas were born out of necessity that spawned creativity. Ideas are often grounded in rigorous research and development and formal education. Other ideas emanate from a person's jobs, interactions with friends, cultural traditions, a slow hunch, or even a passion (or hobby) that consumes many waking hours.

Below, we examine overarching themes expressed by businesspeople regarding the sources of their ideas and how scientific inventions found their way into new products, services, business models, problem solving, and marketing techniques.

> Entrepreneurs have stories
> to share about how they came up with the
> idea that resulted in a successful business.
> For many, the key was being a keen observer
> of people, society, and human behavior.

Imitation

For some entrepreneurs, new ideas build on existing products (or services) that are copied or tweaked in a way that takes an idea to the next level.

Travel is a great way to seek ideas for businesses. Travelers observe people and their changing tastes, which sometimes wend their way into new products. Businesspeople who travel keep their eyes open for ideas worth imitating, which may save time from trying to constantly create new concepts.

Global business management professor Oded Shenkar proposed that "Imitation is faster, cheaper, easier to implement, less risky, and more profitable than innovation—and you can imitate legally and profitably" (2010). The business adage "innovate or die" has gone by the wayside among some risk-averse investors and producers who would rather put their energy into a tried-and-true product, practice, or business model than to start from scratch.

Through mechanisms described in the previous chapter, globalization fuels the imitation model of entrepreneurship as we increasingly live in an interconnected business environment in which we are constantly exposed to each other's ideas and lifestyles.

Invention–Innovation Partnerships

Invention entails the discovery of new science, which usually requires a significant amount of time and money. For some entrepreneurs, envisioning brand-new discoveries that can be turned into lucrative products and/or services is what excites them most.

One inventor, whose products are used today in every office, is **Dr. Spencer Silver**. As a chemist in a research laboratory at 3M, he was charged with inventing an adhesive strong enough to be used in airplane construction. By accident, he invented an adhesive that stuck to surfaces but could easily be peeled off for reuse.

Dr. Silver did not know what to do with his accidental invention, noting "I felt my adhesive was so obviously unique that I began to give seminars throughout 3M in the hope I would spark an idea among its product developers." He was known as "Mr. Persistent." He patented the adhesive (called acrylate copolymer microsphere) in 1972.

Two years later, Art Fry, a 3M chemical engineer who attended one of Dr. Silver's seminars, discovered an application for the adhesive at church choir practice when the slips of paper bookmarking songs in his hymnal kept falling out. So, he applied Dr. Silver's adhesive to create a bookmark that stayed on the page. It worked!

3M eventually introduced the Post-it Notes in 1980, initially in canary yellow, and never stopped selling the popular product. The firm makes a fortune selling billions of Post-it Note pads every year, now offered in 3,000 types of various colors and sizes.

Spencer Silver and Art Fry were inducted into the National Inventors Hall of Fame in 2010, and Dr. Silver received the American Chemical Society's Award for Creative Invention in 1998 (see Silver Obituary, 2021).

Another example of an invention–innovation partnership is **Megvii Technology**. Yin Qi and two friends from China's Tsinghua University created Megvii (standing for *mega vision*) in 2011, the world's largest artificial intelligence (AI) computer vision research institute. The firm became famous for its sophisticated Face++ facial recognition software, which offers 1,000-point facial landmarks to identify a person in a photo or video stream in real time. Megvii has expanded its services to include human body recognition (22-point skeletal points), gait recognition, gesture recognition, emotion recognition, voice recognition, and text recognition. In 2015, Megvii launched Brain++, its deep-learning engine to train algorithms.

Megvii's AI-powered Internet of Things (IoT) products opened the door to multiple applications such as (a) entertaining and interactive online marketing, (b) car owner verification to unlock and start a car and warn drivers of fatigue, and (c) financial payment authentication.

The success of China's Megvii AI computer vision systems exemplifies the value of private for-profit business entrepreneurs partnering with public sector agencies to advance new ideas. The key that enabled Megvii's software to initially recognize the image of an individual person's face was its access to the government's image database of 700 million citizens collected for national identification cards.

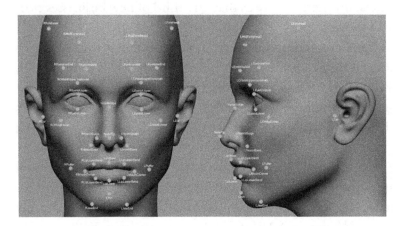

In this partnership, the government provided the facial database and Megvii provided the surveillance cameras and identification software, making the Chinese government a valued customer of Megvii. Perhaps, you too will be able to develop an invention–innovation partnership like Post-it Notes and Megvii to launch your business idea. It is very interesting to see where such partnerships will take us in the future.

Survival Rates

Are you excited about the possibility of being an entrepreneur to get your ideas into the hands of interested customers? Do you have some new ideas that you want to explore? If so, you may be ready to launch your own enterprise by establishing one of the three types of business structures explored in Chapter 3: sole proprietorships, partnerships, and corporations.

But first, let us consider the risks associated with small business development. The U.S. Department of Labor's Bureau of Labor Statistics (BLS) provides valuable data on the survival rates of businesses registered with the U.S. IRS in the United States. The BLS reported in 2023 that among all registered businesses, 68 percent were still in business two years after being registered by the IRS. To some, the fact that more than two-thirds of businesses make it to the two-year mark is encouraging. To others, this statistic reveals that one-third of new businesses close within two years.

There could be myriad reasons why a business would close its doors. On the upside, a person may simply realize that business is not for them and voluntarily closes its doors. Another person may decide to shift gears and start another business in an entirely different industry. Someone else may decide to apply to graduate school and shutter the business during this period of study.

On the downside, a person may not have been as successful in business as anticipated. Perhaps, some uncontrollable factors negatively impinged on the business, as was the case for many owners during the SARS-CoV-2 pandemic from 2020 to 2022. Others may have experienced mild success in business but had not yet reached the financial break-even point, and hence, they were forced to close their businesses.

But, if your business is among the 68 percent of businesses that are still in operation at the two-year mark, what does the future hold? According to the BLS, after five years, half of all businesses remain open. Thus, it seems that five years is the midpoint when, on average, half of businesses succeed and half go out of business.

The BLS further calculates that, on average, 42 percent of businesses in the United States are still operating after seven years. What are some of the factors contributing to business survival? The most important is financial success, followed by managerial success. Other factors, in no particular order, relate to planning, operations, human resources, location, timing, and global capitalism. And, of course, we cannot forget just plain old luck. We can only guess how many hardworking people with great ideas and ample resources come up against hard luck in the world of business through no fault of their own.

Thus, consider carefully the industry in which you would like to establish your new business. The inclusion of data on survival and the abovementioned failure rates is not to discourage you from going into business but rather to give you a heads-up and reminder that business is not for risk-averse individuals, something to consider when setting up your own business.

U.S. Small Business Administration

Before concluding this module on entrepreneurship and small business development, there is one additional important resource to tap. In 1953, the U.S. government established an office to serve small business owners called the U.S. Small Business Administration (SBA). With its headquarters in Washington, DC, plus regional and district offices across the country, the SBA is a valuable resource for those wishing to start and run a small business.

How do you know if you qualify as a small business? The definition is established by the SBA and factors in three components. First, the business cannot dominate an industry or field. Hence, Amazon and Alphabet would not be considered "small" businesses. Second, the SBA sets a cutoff to the number of employees that a business hires to be considered a "small" business. Third, there are caps on the annual receipts (in USD) that a business can bring in to be considered "small."

The caps on the number of employees and total annual receipts vary from industry to industry. Manufacturing and mining firms, for example, qualify as small businesses if they have no more than 500 employees. In contrast, the cutoff for wholesalers is only 100 employees. With regard to sales revenues, the cutoff is $7,50,000 for agricultural business, $7 million for retailers, and $14 million for special trade contractors.

The first step when establishing your own businesses is to check the website www.SBA.gov to determine whether your firm qualifies as a small business. It is potentially valuable if your business qualifies as a "small" business in the eyes of the SBA. If so, you are eligible to attend SBA trainings in the various functional areas of business to help you deepen your knowledge in areas where you could use assistance. Business executives and retirees often offer their services for free to help small business owners get started. Training is offered in a wide range of areas from bookkeeping and accounting to marketing and management.

Another advantage of being considered a "small" business is that you may qualify for special SBA-guaranteed business loans through commercial banks and credit unions to help start and/ or grow your business. Such loans are advantageous in that they require smaller down payments and allow longer repayment periods relative to commercial banks.

"A size standard, which is usually stated in number of employees or average annual receipts, represents the largest size that a business (including its subsidiaries and affiliates) may be to remain classified as a small business for SBA and federal contracting programs. The definition of 'small' varies by industry."

Source: Small Business Administration. www.sba.gov.

Small Business Profile

Every year, the U.S. SBA's Office of Advocacy creates profiles of small businesses at the national and state levels, describing small business activities.

According to the SBA:

The Office of Advocacy's Small Business Profiles are an annual analysis of each state's small business activities. Each profile gathers the latest information from key federal data-gathering agencies to provide a snapshot of small business health and economic activity. This year's profiles report on state economic growth and employment; small business employment, industry composition, and turnover; plus business owner demographics and county-level employment change.

In 2023, the SBA identified a total of 33.3 million small businesses in the United States, representing 99.9 percent of all businesses with payroll. Almost 62 million employees worked for small businesses, representing 46 percent of the private sector workforce.

Other interesting characteristics of the small business sector in the United States include the following:

- 43 percent are owned by women.
- 20 percent are owned by racial minorities.
- 21 percent are owned by immigrants.
- 27 percent are owned by families.
- 24 percent are home based.

The U.S. SBA statistics and reports underscore how rich and varied small businesses are in the United States, suggesting that you will be able to find your place therein.

Wrap Up

With this backdrop on entrepreneurship and small business development, next we will explore the all-important money side of starting and running a business, including financial management, equity financing, and debt financing.

CHAPTER 7

Financial Management

Once you have envisioned a business idea, established yourself as an entrepreneur or secured a job with a business in your industry of interest, and assumed the attendant risks of running a business, what's next? It is time to talk about money in order for you to realize your goal of earning a profit.

There are many financial questions that present themselves at this point in the business process. If you are starting out on your own, you might consider how many years you can support yourself until your business is self-sustaining. If you need money, where do you go? What is this place called Wall Street? How does it work? How do you get people to invest in you and your ideas? If you are going to borrow money, when do you have to repay it? How will you handle growth of your business from a financial perspective? What do people who decide to study finance end up doing on the job?

What Is a Business?
An organization
comprised of people
who produce goods and services
to sell
to earn a profit
distributed to stakeholders

This and the next two chapters will help you decide if the field of finance is for you and, if so, what area(s) of expertise to pursue. In the end, you might decide that you do not necessarily want to become a financial expert, but rather pursue work in another functional area of business. Even so, it helps to know a little about money and banking because we live on a planet where global capitalism impacts every person, business, and corner, no matter how distant or small.

Thus, it pays off to be informed about money and finance. Every business needs money to succeed, be they large transcontinental corporations, mid-sized established businesses, or new small enterprises. We need money to start a business, stay in business, and grow a business. Money is the oil that greases the wheels of business.

We define business as an organization comprised of people who produce goods and services to be sold in order to earn a profit distributed to stakeholders. The finance functional area gets to the heart of earning a profit, which is where we begin.

> It helps to know a little about money and banking because we live on a planet where global capitalism impacts every person, business, and corner, no matter how distant or small.

Careers in Finance

One of the benefits of becoming a financial expert is the array of jobs available across industries. In the private for-profit world of business, finance is a requirement to succeed as a CEO. This was not necessarily the case in the past when an individual who was knowledgeable about a particular product or service could establish and run a business without having a lot of financial know-how, which could be handled by associates skilled in finance. This is no longer the case. Every CEO today starts the day combing through financial data pertaining to one's business and industry. Hence, studying finance is a must for those seeking to be a chief executive one day.

Chief Financial Officers (CFOs) are also responsible for the financial functioning of business. The CFO works non-stop on matters related to money, banking, and financing of the business. That said, given the data intensity of business today, I learned being a CFO that we are privy to an enormous amount of information that goes beyond just finance, to include strategy, operations, human resources, and logistics. Thus, while overseeing the finance department, the CFO plays a controlling role in broader aspects of a business. This is why the median pay for a CFO employed by an S&P 500 company in 2023 was $4.7 million, unless you are Walmart's CFO John David Rainey, who was the highest-paid CFO that year at nearly $40 million.

Banks also hire people with expertise in finance, including bank presidents, bank officers, and consumer credit officers. The best way to begin a career as a financial executive in a bank is to start as a bank teller, who is responsible for the daily handling of cash and frontline customer needs. In the investing industry, financial experts fill positions such as financial analysts, financial planners, and investment account executives. These experts are responsible for handling other people's money as well as the investment house's own proprietary investments.

Accountants are trained financial experts who perform necessary bookkeeping, tax filings, and financial reporting for businesses of all types. Professional accountants have passed a state examination to hold a CPA license. Comptrollers are also trained accountants as are forensic accountants, who specialize in financial fraud detection and more.

Financial Management Process

If you are considering becoming a financial manager for a business, what would your job entail? In a nutshell, the financial management process proceeds in four steps, as follows.

Step #1: Establish Clear Financial Goals With Your Client

Step #1 requires spending time with your clients, usually members of the board of directors, the CEO, and other senior executives, to clarify exactly what they want to see happen in the short-term vis-à-vis the firm's finances. Is this a year when new facilities will be built? Is an M&A envisioned? Is a division shut down in the works? Is there a specific return on investment desired by the directors?

The financial goals must be realistic, which is your job to ensure. Big thinking is great; however, our job as financial managers is to be sure that the goals are achievable from a money perspective, which demands tough conversations and careful deliberations. Securing consensus on the short-term financial goals among the executives may take several meetings over a long period of time. The extra effort to ensure that everyone is operating on the same page is well worth the energy; otherwise, there could be a lack of clarity across the business as to where the firm is headed.

Step #2: Prepare a Draft Budget

Once the short-term financial goals are agreed upon, Step #2 of the financial process is for you to prepare a draft budget. This requires seeking detailed estimates of the projected income over an agreed-upon period (e.g., one calendar year) alongside projected expenditures during the same period. As the financial manager, you may have to train staff in the various divisions of the business on how to come up with budget estimates, a job that will pay off in subsequent accounting cycles.

Step #3: Conduct a Budget Analysis

This step entails analyzing the data collected in Step #2 and determining whether the business will have sufficient funds to realize its goals over the specific period in question. It is important to stress that your budget analysis will only be as good as the data that were provided by division managers on projected income and expenditures. This is where it pays off to work closely with division managers and teach them how to devise solid estimates.

The answer to the question posed in Step #3 (will the business have sufficient funds to realize its goals?) is binary. If yes, you are concluding that to the best of your knowledge and data, the business will be able to meet its financial goals for the period in question. In this case, your job is to present the findings to the executives and carefully monitor the books week in and week out to be sure that the actual income and expenditures do not veer far from the projected income and expenditures.

Step #4: Consider Possible Financing Mechanisms

If the answer to the question posed in Step #3 is no, then you are concluding that the business will not, in all likelihood, be able to meet its financial goals, which leads us to Step #4: consider possible financing mechanisms. Before you share the bad news with the executives, I recommend that you devise some ideas as to how the business might achieve its financial goals. After possible financing mechanisms are discussed and a financial plan is approved, you and your financial management division will secure the necessary financing and monitor the progress benchmarked to the financial goals established in Step #1.

Wrap Up

The next two chapters will explore in-depth financial mechanisms to help finance business activities grouped into two options: equity financing and debt financing.

CHAPTER 8

Equity Finance

All business owners need money—known as financing—to establish a firm, to operate daily, and to grow in whatever ways the owner deems best.

Two of the most common forms of financing are **equity** and **debt**. The value of equity financing is that the money people invest in your business does not come with a promise that it be repaid. Debt financing, in contrast, requires repayment with some type of compensating interest, as negotiated. This chapter provides examples of equity financing, followed by examples of debt financing in the next chapter.

What Is a Business?
An organization
comprised of people
who produce goods and services
to sell
to earn a profit
distributed to stakeholders

Equity finance is a form of financing in which you convince other people to invest money directly into your business. This money could be used for myriad purposes, ranging from building a new office to developing a new product, paying off debt, purchasing equipment, hiring workers, buying inventory, or paying off accounts receivable.

Securing equity finance requires aggressive fundraising on your part as the owner or the responsible party representing someone else's business.

Anyone with money to invest is a possible source of equity financing, such as other business owners interested in your firm, individual investors, or the owners of the business itself.

Equity investors own a part of your business and expect to be financially rewarded if the business is a financial success. Let's look at five types of equity finance common to business: owner's equity, shareholder's equity, retained earnings, venture capital (VC), and assets.

Type 1: Owner's Equity

Owner's equity is a straightforward, quick, and simple way to raise money for a business. This is money that an owner, say the person who started the business, puts into the business to get it up and running or to expand. It is common for people starting their own business to have saved up enough money to invest in the start-up of a new firm for an initial period of time. If the firm is a partnership, each partner could invest owner's equity in the business, as needed.

It is important to note that any money put into the business in the form of owner's equity is not a loan to be repaid to that person. The owners are investing their own money with the assumption that the business will be successful and reap rewards in the form of significant profits and job security, for example, in the future.

Type 2: Shareholder's Equity

Shareholder's equity takes form through the sale of shares of stock in a business. Each stock is sold to an investor who pays a specific price per share. The money the investor pays for the stock serves as shareholder equity that the business may use as needed.

Closed Versus Open

Not all businesses can legally sell stock. Corporations and limited liability partnerships have the advantage of being able to issue and sell stock to raise funds. If you decide to set up your business as a corporation, you must decide whether your firm will be closed or open. A **closed** business is one in which the ownership of the firm is privately held by the owners and a small number of private investors. The public is not allowed to purchase shares in a closed corporation.

In contrast, if you want anybody to be able to invest in your business and acquire shareholder equity, then you will opt to establish your business as an **open** corporation, also known as a publicly traded corporation. In this case, you must choose an exchange where the buying and selling of stocks takes place through brokers and traders. Famous exchanges include the New York Stock Exchange (owned by Intercontinental Exchange), Nasdaq, Japan Exchange Group, Shanghai Stock Exchange, Hong Kong Stock Exchange, Shenzhen Stock Exchange, London Stock Exchange, Euronext in Europe, TMX Group in Canada, and Deutsche Börse in Germany.

If you decide to become an open corporation, whom can you solicit to invest in your business through the purchase of your stock? In today's world of finance, the majority of stockholders are institutional investors, that is, other businesses that invest money in a specific firm via a stock exchange. Examples of institutional investors are bank trusts, mutual funds, hedge funds, endowments, insurers, and pension funds. A minority of stocks held today are purchased by individuals who invest their personal money in stocks, known as retail investors. Almost 80 percent of the stock of corporations listed in the S&P 500 index today is owned by institutional investors, with the remaining is owned by individuals.

Common Versus Preferred

Why would a person spend their hard-earned money on a stock that comes with no promise to repay the money invested? Usually, investors buy stocks sold at a price per share they believe will increase over and above what they paid initially. Thus, when it comes time to cash in, the person will realize a capital gain.

The very first time a business allows the public to buy its stock is called an **initial public offering** (IPO), also known as "going public." Prior to an IPO, the business must decide what type of stock it will sell. One of the main things businesses will decide is whether to sell common shares and preferred shares. The difference is key to knowing who will be invited to the corporation's annual meeting.

If your business sells stock to the public, it is required by U.S. law to hold a stockholder's meeting at least once a year and to notify stockholders beforehand. The meeting is a way to learn about new ideas, products, or strategies envisioned by the board of directors and senior executives. It is also a place where shareholders can pose questions of the owners and operators of the business. Anyone who holds common or preferred shares is invited to attend the annual shareholders meeting and will receive a formal invitation along with salient items to be discussed.

At the annual meeting, stockholders will be presented with specific items that require a vote, such as deciding who will serve on the board of directors and other matters pertaining to governance, operations, and business policy. Who is allowed to vote on such matters? Only common shareholders. Thus, while preferred shareholders may attend the annual shareholders meeting, they are nonvoting shareholders.

What then makes preferred shares *preferred*? One advantage of holding preferred shares is the preferential claim to business assets and earnings in the event, for example, of a bankruptcy. In this instance, a business will sell off its assets for payout to various stakeholders. First to be paid are bond holders, followed by other creditors, then preferred shareholders, and lastly common shareholders.

One of the topics of great concern each year among shareholders is the amount of money the business will distribute to shareholders in the event the business is profitable. Such distributions are known as **dividends**. Both common and preferred shareholders are eligible for dividend payments, but no one is guaranteed to be paid dividends.

Only the board of directors can determine whether a firm will distribute dividends to shareholders and, if so, the amount of the dividend. At the annual meeting, a representative of the board of directors may tell shareholders of its intention to pay dividends at the end of the coming year if profit targets are met (or exceeded), but the board has the right to change its mind in the interest of the business. Dividend payments are paid either quarterly or semiannually.

In sum, common shareholders are invited to the annual shareholders meeting, may vote on issues presented, and are eligible for dividends. In contrast, preferred shareholders are invited to the annual shareholder's meeting and are eligible for dividends but hold nonvoting shares.

Type 3: Retained Earnings

In addition to owner's equity and shareholder's equity, a business also may raise equity capital through retained earnings. At the end of each year (e.g., calendar year, fiscal year), your accountants will present to you and your partners a summary of all financial activities that transpired. The accountants will calculate the total revenues that came into the business throughout the year from all sources. They will then subtract the total costs accrued throughout the year by all expense categories. The balance is your business' annual net profit.

Before you start thinking about all the things you will do with those profits, your accountant will remind you of the pledge made to pay dividends to shareholders in the event you are an open corporation. Once dividends have been paid, the remaining sum of money is called *retained earnings*.

Retained earnings are a form of equity financing that you may invest in your business. It is a simple and direct way to raise money quickly to cover financial needs. And it is cost-free as any money left over after dividends have been paid are yours to keep or reinvest in your business.

Of note are historical trends in the dividend payout ratio (percentage of corporate profits paid out as dividends) by publicly traded corporations in the United States, which directly impact retained earnings. From 1900 to the 1970s, an average of two-thirds of profits were paid out in the form of dividends, thus encouraging investors to put their money into shares of stock with the assumption that significant dividend payments would be received at year's end. During the 1980s and 1990s, only one-third of profits were paid out in dividends, on average. During and immediately following the Great Recession (2007–2009), many corporations stopped paying dividends altogether. The collapse of the dividend was a notable financial occurrence.

Post-2012, however, some of the major transnational corporations slowly resumed paying dividends, albeit at historically low levels. The result is more cash for use as retained earnings and fewer investors seeking dividend payments on their shareholder equity investments. During the 2010s, part of this cash windfall was used by businesses to buy back their own stock. An estimated $6 trillion was spent on stock repurchases over the decade ending 2021 and some $4 trillion on dividends. In so doing, many corporations demonstrated a preference for moving away from being open corporations (with stock available for purchase by the public) to being closed corporations (with stock privately held).

In the 2020s, the average payout ratio is 31 percent. With profit margins elevated and cash flowing, the question is whether firms might redirect funds into paying special dividends moving forward.

Type 4: Venture Capital

VC is money raised from wealthy investors, be they institutions or individuals, who hope their investments will yield significant short-term profits. This type of equity financing is unlike shareholder's equity in that you are not selling a tangible stock that serves as an investor's claim on the business. Nor is the money coming from a founder or owner who has a vested long-term interest in the firm. Venture capitalists may know very little about you or your business except a notion that whatever goods or services you are producing may pay off handsomely one day soon. But they have money and want to invest quickly in technology novelties.

As a result, new small technology firms are able to raise large quantities of money from venture capitalists seeking the next big invention, rather than raising money through stock offerings. The result is that VC-funded firms can stay private for long periods of time and avoid IPOs (stocks), lengthening the time before venture capitalists can get their money out. The longer the wait to sell stocks, the higher the risk for the venture capitalist equity investors.

What might a venture capitalist want in return for giving a business its money? Some might demand ownership in the funded firm, such as becoming a limited partner. Some might want privately held preferred stock (with an option to convert to common stock) and a promise of being first in the queue to sell those shares when the business makes its IPO or is bought out in an M&A.

Type 5: Assets

The fifth and final example of equity finance in this module is a last resort. If your firm really needs cash and has had no success fundraising through owner's equity, shareholder's equity, retained earnings, or VC, you are left with the last resort, which is to sell the assets owned by your business.

I left this type of equity financing for last because, as a rule, you do not want to rely on selling assets to keep your business moving forward. In fact, it may be very difficult to operate fully if you start selling assets such as trucks, buildings, and inventory. However, if you are in dire straits and want one more push to raise equity financing to propel your business forward, go ahead and sell some of your assets and use the money in this time of need. After all, that is why we have assets.

Notable Trends

There are two notable trends when it comes to equity finance mechanisms.

First, in the United States, fewer firms are deciding to sell shares to the general public. In 1996, there were 7,322 businesses listing their stock on public exchanges. By 2023, that number was down to 5,704 (2,272 domestic and international companies listed on the New York Stock Exchange and 3,432 on the Nasdaq). More businesses are avoiding IPOs. Why? Because there are new sources of equity financing from wealthy individuals, private equity firms, and venture capitalists who are willing to provide businesses with capital.

New and highly valued firms are staying private longer, making it difficult to buy into a business you deem to be a potential winner unless you are privy to a private placement (or sale) of stock to a small number of chosen investors.

The founder of Uber, Travis Kalanick, famously touted, "I say we are going to IPO as late as humanly possible. It'll be one day before my employees and significant others come to my office with pitchforks and torches" (Axel Springer NOAH Berlin Conference 2015). Kalanick indicated that he did not need shareholder equity for Uber, which was then valued at $41 billion, almost four times the $11 billion value of the entire taxi industry in the United States. After Kalanick was ousted as CEO in 2017, Uber's board of directors held an IPO at the New York Stock Exchange on May 10, 2019, yielding the business $8.1 billion in equity capital.

Founders of businesses feel less pressure to go public today. The reason is because there are plenty of private funders willing to invest in them. By the middle of 2023, for example, private equity funds managed $8.2 trillion, more than twice the amount in 2018, partly explaining the so-called disappearing stock market (*The Economist* 2024).

A second notable trend in equity financing is the sale of **nonvoting shares** by a corporation. Nonvoting shares allow the founders to retain control of business operations, governance, and decision making while at the same time raising equity. The advent of stock with zero-voting rights (e.g., "C" class shares) is not without controversy. In 2017, S&P and FTSE Russell said they would no longer include firms with multiple share class structures (including nonvoting shares) in their benchmark indices. In a turn of events, on April 17, 2023, the S&P Dow Jones Indices announced that it will allow existing multiple share index constituents to remain in the S&P indices, a departure from its previous restrictions.

The Securities and Exchange Commission overseeing equity finance in the U.S. noted that the practice of shifting to nonvoting shares "raises the prospect that control over public companies, and ultimately of Main Street's retirement savings, will be forever held by a small, elite group of corporate insiders" (WSJ 2018). One idea being discussed to limit outsized founder voting power is to establish a rule whereby businesses must retire their dual-share structure after a limited number of years rather than upon the death of the founder or longtime controlling shareholder.

Wrap Up

Never a dull moment in high finance!

CHAPTER 9

Debt Finance

When looking for money to finance your business, you have many options. In our society, it is easy to think immediately about borrowing money to realize your ambitions. While debt can be a solid solution to your financial concerns, it is not the best place to start looking for money. Hence, we began our discussion about financing with equity capital in the previous chapter. You may want to fully consider the options available to you and your business in the form of equity capital, including owner's equity, shareholder's equity, VC, and retained earnings, before venturing into debt financing.

If you still need money, then it might be time to consider borrowing. There are times when debt is the best option, but only if you realize the risks involved and can make good on your promise to repay the money owed.

Following is a discussion of short-term debt, which must be repaid within one year, and long-term debt, repayable in more than one year, depending on the agreed-upon terms. By the end of this chapter, you will have a good sense of the pros and cons of going into debt to finance your business start-up, ongoing operations, and/or growth strategy.

Short-Term Debt Financing

Short-term debt financing is borrowed money that must be repaid within a year depending on the agreement made between the borrower and the lender.

Type 1: Secured Debt

The first type of short-term debt is called **secured debt**. In the event that someone is considering giving you a loan for your business, you may be asked to present the lender with some kind of collateral that will make the lender whole if the borrowed money is not repaid in full.

Think about what you own that you would be willing to put on the table—and possibly lose—in the event you default on the loan. For example, do you own a car that you could put up as collateral? Do you own a house? Do you own any inventory or a building you could use as collateral? Determining what form of collateral will meet the needs of the potential lender is a matter of negotiation. Put your best foot forward when making a case for your credit worthiness. But do not be offended if the lender decides it is vital for you to post collateral in return for a short-term loan.

> There are times when debt is the best option, but only if you realize the risks involved and can make good on your promise to repay the money owed.

Type 2: Unsecured Debt

Every lender is different. Not all require collateral, a decision based on a host of factors such as a borrower's credit score, track record repaying previous loans, and income history. If you do not look like a financial risk, you may not have to post collateral to secure a short-term loan. The lender may be willing to issue you an **unsecured short-term loan** with no required collateral.

One example of unsecured short-term debt financing is **trade credit**. Trade credit is an excellent way to delay payment to a supplier for 30–60 days. Trade credit occurs when a business regularly orders from a supplier merchandise to be sold in, for example, a retail store. Rather than paying the supplier the moment the merchandise is delivered, trade credit provides the business with a short window of time to come up with the money to pay its supplier. In the United States, more than three-quarters of businesses have established trade credit agreements with their suppliers.

Let's examine how deliveries work without trade credit. Suppose you own a retail store that receives regular deliveries of goods from your supplier that will be displayed and sold in your store. On the day merchandise is delivered to the store, you will examine the merchandise, sign for the delivery, and pay the driver an agreed-upon amount of money for the merchandise. That completes the transaction.

If you and the supplier have a trade credit agreement, the process changes. On the day the merchandise is delivered, you examine the contents, sign for the delivery, and receive an invoice from the supplier listing all items delivered and the amount of money owed. On the invoice, you will see a statement that will look something like the following: 2/10, net 60. What do these numbers mean? The 2 means that you will be able to deduct 2 percent of the total amount due if you pay for the delivery within 10 days. Otherwise, you must pay the full amount for the delivered merchandise within 60 days.

In other words, the supplier is offering you a 2 percent savings if you pay for today's delivery before the 60-day trade credit payment date. Trade credit is a wonderful short-term debt financing mechanism because it gives you time to sell the merchandise and earn the money to repay the supplier. In other words, trade credit is free money! No interest is due on the money owed.

Some trade credit short-term debt financing agreements are for 30 days, the longest is usually 60 days, depending on what you and your supplier agree upon. If you are able to take advantage of the discount offered by the supplier and pay before the end of the 30-to-60-day window, by all means do so. Every little bit of savings helps.

A second example of unsecured short-term debt is a **promissory note**. What if you need more than 60 days to repay a supplier for the merchandise you will be selling in your store? You could negotiate a promissory note, which is a promise to repay the lender within an agreed-upon period of time. Promissory notes require repayment in no longer than 365 days (i.e., 12 months), as negotiated. This gives you considerably more time to sell the merchandise in your store and earn the money to repay the supplier relative to a trade credit arrangement.

In return for having more time to repay the supplier than trade credit, a promissory note requires that you pay the money owed *with interest* accrued over the entire repayment period. This makes sense given that the supplier needs some type of monetary compensation for loaning you the money until payment is received.

Take your time negotiating the details of a promissory note repayment plan and put the terms of the agreement in writing to be reviewed and signed by both the lender and the borrower. There is no such thing as a verbal promissory note. There is no such thing as a handshake deal with a promissory note.

A promissory note is a legal and tradable instrument, binding you to pay the money owed within the agreed-upon repayment period plus an agreed-upon rate of interest. The lender in this case does not require the borrower to post collateral, hence promissory notes are another example of unsecured debt.

A third type of short-term debt is an **unsecured bank loan**. One of the things that you will want to know when shopping for a banker for your business is whether the bank provides business loans and the specific terms therein. If the bank issues short-term business loans, how much time does a business owner have to repay the loan? How much interest would a borrower have to pay the bank for the loan? How often will the business have to make payments on a short-term unsecured loan? All these questions need be to be explored and negotiated by the borrower and lender.

There are times when a banker may require you to provide some type of assurance that you will repay the loan. Some banks will only issue secured loans. In the absence of collateral, a bank might require that you have a certain amount of money in a business savings or checking account with the same bank. As with all short-term loans, the bank will expect repayment within 12 months, per the agreed-upon terms of the loan.

A fourth type of short-term unsecured debt is **commercial paper**. Commercial paper is borrowed money that must be repaid in no longer than 12 months. It is also a promissory note, meaning a promise to be repaid, without posting collateral.

Commercial paper is a debt-financing tool commonly used by large businesses, especially corporations, to raise money quickly. A business may need, for example, money to fill a cash flow gap in the months leading up to the winter holiday season and could sell commercial paper to secure sufficient funds to increase its inventory. Commercial paper also could be sold to raise funds to pay large accounts receivable, short-term liabilities, and even payroll, depending on the needs of the firm at a certain point in time. Commercial paper is usually not used for fixed assets (e.g., a new office or plant).

In order to raise short-term commercial paper funds, a business posts a notice of its intention to sell its "paper" to the general public and/or other businesses. Buyers of commercial paper include wealthy individuals, money market funds, financial institutions, and other large corporations seeking short-term investments. Usually, commercial paper will be repaid in less than or equal to 270 days (i.e., 9 months). The average length of commercial paper debt instrument in the United States is 30 days. No collateral is required to be posted.

Commercial paper became very popular in the United States beginning in the 1990s. The value of outstanding commercial paper was $500 billion in 1991 and rose to $1.58 trillion by 2005, peaking at $1.78 trillion in 2007, just before the Wall Street financial crisis. By mid-2024, the value of outstanding commercial paper was $1.2 trillion.

The difference between commercial paper and standard promissory notes is the manner in which lenders are compensated. Most firms sell commercial paper in lots of $100,000, which would be the "face value" of the note payable in, say, 30 days. However, on the day the commercial paper is sold, the business will receive from the lender less than $100,000, which is the "par value." The difference between the face value and the par value is the money the lender earns by lending money through the sale of commercial paper.

This form of short-term debt financing is thus considered a noninterest-bearing note because the lender does not technically earn interest on the loan, but rather is compensated by the difference between the agreed-upon par value (the dollar amount loaned) and the face value (the dollar amount repaid).

Long-Term Debt Financing

In addition to short-term debt instruments (i.e., secured and unsecured), businesses might seek long-term debt financing for projects that are more ambitious and may take considerable time to reap the anticipated financial rewards. Long-term debt financing is borrowed money that must be repaid with interest in more than one year, depending on what is negotiated between the lender and the borrower.

Following are two types of long-term debt financing instruments: bank loans and corporate bonds.

Long-Term Bank Loans

Long-term bank loans are similar to short-term bank loans in that they provide needed financial capital to businesses that promise to repay the loan with interest. Each bank sets the terms of its loans, including the amount of money it will lend a borrower (the principal amount), the length of time a borrower has to repay the loan (the repayment period), and the amount of interest a borrower must pay the lender as compensation.

Commercial banks and cooperative banks usually set interest rates in sync with monetary policies set by the Federal Reserve, the central bank of the United States. Interest rates also will reflect the perceived financial risk of each potential borrower. If you seek a long-term bank loan, the bank will conduct a credit check on your firm's creditworthiness before determining the terms of the loan. Rarely will a bank require collateral to issue a long-term business loan.

Corporate Bonds

A second source of long-term debt financing for a business is through the sale of a corporate bond. This is a common mechanism used by big firms to raise large amounts of money, at times billions of dollars, from other businesses, institutional investors, individual investors, and sovereign governments.

Suppose you have saved some money and would like to invest it in a business that you see is growing and/or holds tremendous potential. For whatever reason, you do not want to buy stock in that business, which would involve an equity transaction. Instead, you decide to loan the business some of your money by buying a corporate bond. As a result, you expect to be repaid in an agreed-upon amount of time and to receive interest payments on the money you have loaned through the bond sale.

Corporate bonds are long-term investment vehicles that can be held for 10, 20, and sometimes 30 years. This is a long time to have your money tied up if you are a corporate bond holder. The longer the time period for the bond, the more interest you can expect to earn on the money you lend to the business. As a corporate bond holder, you are now a creditor, meaning you have a claim on the business's assets in the event that the firm goes bankrupt.

Corporate bonds are a steady source of debt financing for corporations. Total outstanding global corporate bond debt reached a new high of $33 trillion at the end of 2023, one-third of which were issued by U.S. businesses.

Wrap Up

These are very interesting times for debt financing given the end of 14 years of near-record low interest rates to 2022. Between 2022 and 2024, the Federal Reserve raised its benchmark interest rate 11 times. Lending to businesses has become more attractive for creditors.

A trend to watch is the changing role of **private equity firms**. As the name suggests, such firms provide equity capital to businesses in exchange for the potential to make great sums in the event of an IPO or other payouts as negotiated. In recent years, however, private equity firms have aggressively become lenders to businesses in need of money for M&As. With so much money-chasing buyout deals in the 2010s, some of the traditional lenders (e.g., banks) stopped lending for buyouts, and private equity firms stepped in.

The shift is notable: the value of traditional retail bank loan funds dropped in 2023, while private credit funds rose from approximately $1 trillion in 2020 to $1.5 trillion in 2024. At present, hybrid financing is popular whereby debt is jointly provided by private creditors and retail bankers. Such joint financing may result in private equity firms providing both equity financing and debt financing simultaneously, sometimes to the same businesses—a risky strategy.

In the end, it is valuable to understand the various types of equity and debt-financing mechanisms available to new and established businesses in order to weigh the risks and benefits of seeking outside money to support your business goals.

CHAPTER 10

Digitization

In the last two decades, digital transactions have exploded. Businesses are able to amass large quantities of data through apps (that comprise two-thirds of internet traffic), ecommerce purchases, social commerce (mix of online commerce and social media), mobile robotic devices (phones, earbuds, headsets, tablets), beacons, sensors, multimedia links, and other telecommunication tools used around the world 24/7.

As a result, business schools offer degree programs in a new *functional area of business* known as data science, data analytics, data mining, and big data. Students learn to use advanced digital tools that allow businesses to collect, store, sort, and analyze data for decision making, advertising, and social engineering.

Because of advances in data mining on all aspects of our lives in the first quarter of the 21st century, businesses have the raw materials to influence societal behavior at a level that would make the Ad Men and Ad Women of the 20th century. Previously, advertisers relied on "broadcasting" their messages in the hopes of capturing the attention of potential customers. Today, digitization enables advertisers to microtarget an individual likely to buy their product or service. Thus, a great deal of money has been invested by businesses in data collection and analysis.

Digitization is a game changer in today's business environment and worth our attention. This chapter will explore how digitization grew out of advances in computer hardware, software, and wireless connectivity. We will study businesses that have created far-reaching networked digital supply chains that connect businesses directly with individual customers through robotic devices. We will consider how computer algorithms microtarget and nudge customers using predictive analysis.

We will look at competition in the latest microprocessing chips and hyperscale data centers triggering the generative AI boom. We will examine microchip sensors and beacons used by retailers to directly access customer mobile devices for merchandising and pricing information. We will consider how data collection business translates into profits.

If you are curious about our digitized world, understanding this new and dynamic functional area of business is the place to start your exploration.

The Cloud

To understand digitization, we need to return to the mid-1990s with the advent of what is now called cloud computing and its pioneer Bill Gates, founder of Microsoft in Silicon Valley, California. After making a fortune selling Microsoft hardware and software, Gates turned his attention to the trove of data his firm had amassed. He considered how his customers might access data that Microsoft stored on their network of servers.

Gates came up with a user-friendly term, *the cloud,* for customers to envision a floating cloud of data in the sky that could be accessed from any location, regardless of where computers, servers, and customers were physically located. He announced that users could now store and access their data that sat in "the cloud" wirelessly through web browsers (e.g., Firefox Mozilla, Microsoft Internet Explorer, Google Chrome, Safari).

The term *cloud computing* stuck. As Microsoft's customer databases grew, so did the size of the cloud of data collected from all digitally connected activities. Once society adopted the use of handheld mobile devices, more data was streamed into the cloud.

Data storage and computing, however, are not cheap. Microsoft pays dearly for huge networks of servers that store customer data. Initially, customers were able to access some of their personal data from the MS cloud for free. The next step was to figure out how to use customer data to make money, specifically how to *monetize* the data collected through customers' online and offline activities.

One way was for Microsoft to post suggestions to its customers, pointing to other products that a person might be interested in buying based on past data collected online. From here, computer scientists started writing predictive algorithms that followed some type of logic whereby if a consumer purchased products A, B, and C, then they might be interested in purchasing products D, E, and F. The strategy was a success.

Data collection and predictive analysis proved to be a lucrative business model for cloud platforms, prompting other large firms to create their own clouds with customer-based data. Google founders, Sergey Brin and Larry Page, saw the vast potential and purchased the YouTube video-streaming site in 2006 for $1.65 billion. Mark Zuckerberg, founder of Facebook, realized that he was sitting on a gold mine of data collected on three billion people across the planet who post data on Facebook accounts. Internet Service Providers (ISPs), to whom users pay monthly fees to access the Net, realized that they too had enormous stores of data unique to each customer, which could be monetized. Large retail stores also saw the value of the "cloud" of data they collected on every purchase made by every customer who shopped at their stores.

The next piece of the puzzle was figuring out where users were located. When **geolocation tracking** was embedded into mobile devices, digital platforms knew who was carrying the mobile device, detailed demographics on the person, how they spent their time and money, the person's online and offline behaviors, and now their specific location and movements.

Digital platforms became a fast-growing, lucrative business. The question became: who might pay for such consumer data.

Enter the Marketers

This is where the marketers entered the picture. Historically, marketers have done their best to disseminate product advertisements to capture peoples' attention via radio and TV broadcasts, print publications, billboards, and other media. While an expensive proposition, this strategy was perceived as necessary to reach a broad pool of potential buyers.

But what if marketers could purchase a list of names of people who exhibited certain traits and behaviors and, hence, might be ready customers? Such a list would save businesses lots of money in advertising. The key is finding the right "cloud" of data. **Data brokers** began serving as intermediaries between data collectors and advertisers. Turns out that marketers are willing to pay data brokers dearly for the kind of data that could be used to micro-target specific customers.

Data brokers set up **advertising exchanges** whereby advertisers engage in a real-time bidding process for the right to pay for and send a customized advertisement to a user. Each time someone opens a mobile website or app with ad space, for example, the ad exchange notifies advertisers that a pair of eyeballs is looking at a computer screen. Advertisers engage in a quick bidding process. The winner pays a fee to the exchange and posts a customized ad to the user. Real-time bidding is obviously valuable not only for the winner of the bid but also for the losers. Why? Because ad exchanges pass information about the user to all bidders, even those who did not win the bid.

Data collection has expanded beyond computerized screens. Automobiles are a data broker's dream. Each time a person turns on an automobile, a host of data points are collected on the car, the driver, and the other passengers. This is possible through built-in navigation systems and mobile phone apps designed to provide vehicle navigation services.

According to Comparitech, connected cars collect between 25 and 383 gigabytes of data an hour of which 50 to 70 percent is sent to the manufacturer's cloud (Schamotta 2024). To see how much data is collected in your car, go to Privacy4Car's *Vehicle Privacy Report* and enter the vehicle identification number (VIN).

Cars come loaded with sensors picking up data. For example, automobile tires have a tire pressure monitoring sensor (TPMS) that broadcasts a unique identifier tied to a particular vehicle (Tau 2024). This is how the car's computer knows the pressure of each tire. Because the sensor is not encrypted, anyone with an antenna can capture transmissions from someone else's car. On many U.S. roads today, there is no longer any ways to legally drive in anonymity. Our location will be captured and documented by radio-frequency devices.

The same holds for all other connected devices such as car key fobs, smoke detectors, robotic vacuums, tap-to-pay credit cards, and any app-enabled transaction. For this reason, people sometimes put their smaller connected devices into "faraday bags" to block being tracked. Some may see this data collection as an invasion of privacy, but it has proven to be a worthy business strategy that you should know about.

Harnessing microdata directly from customers gets easier day by day and screen by screen. A new advertising data ecosystem has emerged that relies on apps, geolocation identification, and ad exchange data. Anyone in marketing today needs to know what's going on!

Operations of Digital Platforms

Each year, the management consulting firm Gartner compiles a list of the leading cloud platforms globally. In 2024, the biggest firms by revenues were as follows:

1: Amazon Web Services
2: Microsoft Azure
3: Oracle Cloud Infrastructure
4: Google Cloud Platform
5: IBM Cloud Services
6: Alibaba Cloud
7: Tencent Cloud
8: Huawei Cloud

These eight businesses control 97 percent of the total infrastructure that supports the global cloud platform industry today. They offer clients so-called Platform-as-a-service (Paas) and Infrastructure-as-a-service (Iaas), including data storage, networking, computing, automation, and application management on a global scale.

To be effective, data professionals rely on large quantities of data collected from human activities; fast chips to process the data; and enormous data centers to store, process, and route the data.

Computer Chips

The growing hunger for digitally woven bulk data by businesses and governments, coupled with society's nascent fascination with AI calculations, means increasing demand for computer chips with greater speed and capacity.

The current leader in the computer chip race is **Nvidia** (pronounced *en-vid-iya*), cofounded by Jen-Hsun (Jensen) Huang

in 1993 in Santa Clara, California. Nvidia sells an advanced graphics processing unit (GPU), a circuit board with a powerful microchip at its core. GPUs were originally designed to process videogame graphics, but are now in demand for AI applications. Amazon Web Services, Microsoft Azure, and Google Cloud rely on Nvidia for GPU chips, networking equipment, and software tools to power AI supercomputing factories and data centers.

On June 18, 2024, Nvidia momentarily became the world's most valuable company at $3.33 trillion. This made Nvidia's CEO, Jen-Hsun Huang, the 11th richest person with a net worth of $119 billion (Financial Times 2024). Huang named his firm Nvidia as a play on the Latin word *invidia*, meaning "envy." Nvidia's new chip architecture—with a gross profit margin approaching 70 percent—is the envy of the supercomputer industry today (Witt 2023).

To process data faster, AI chips are getting bigger. Nvidia's state-of-the-art GUP graphics chip is about the size of a postage stamp. The next-generation AI chips might be the size of a dinner plate. Some of the firms competing with this industry leader include Advanced Micro Devices, Cerebras, Groq, Hailo, Taalas, Tenstorre, Graphcore, and the Silicon Valley large digital platforms. The challenge with AI is getting all the interconnected chips to work together with clever routing software to move data quickly. Speed is key to boosting performance.

Hyperscale Data Centers

Also key is the size of data storage facilities, now referred to as hyperscale cloud computing data centers that can range in size from 400,000 sq. ft. to two million sq. ft.

The greatest concentration of hyperscale data centers is in Northern Virginia through which an estimated 70 percent of global digital internet traffic is routed (Tau 2024). Historically, this region offered a robust fiber optic network and plentiful open land located close to electrical substations and electrical transmission lines capable of powering data facilities. These centers also require large quantities of fresh water to cool down the servers. Between 2019 and 2024, water consumption in Northern Virginia's "data center alley" rose by two-thirds (Hodgson 2024).

In addition to the draw of supporting infrastructure, Amazon Web Services selected Virginia for its data centers because of its proximity to the Pentagon, its biggest data customer. Microsoft did the same, also to serve its clients in the federal government.

Data centers—which can top 75 feet in height—are constructed on many acres of land, where hundreds of thousands of data servers run round-the-clock to collect, store, save, and process consumer, government, and business data. An estimated 5,000 large data facilities operate in the United States.

Outside of the United States, Singapore and Malaysia are major hubs for hyperscale data centers because of their expansive fiber optic data cable infrastructure. After a three-year moratorium on new data center investments in Singapore between 2019 and 2022, "Singapore made a surprise announcement [in

May 2024] that it would free up more power for data centre expansion. The move came as the chief executives of Nvidia, Google, Microsoft and others have been swinging by neighbouring Malaysia in recent months pledging billions in data center investment" (Ruehl 2024).

The physicality of big data collection is testing the limits of the infrastructural grid in local municipalities the world over, something we need to understand if we are going into this industry. As demand for computing power grows to run generative AI networks, firms will have to overhaul and vastly expand existing data centers. *Financial Times* reported that over the next four to five years, it could take up to $1 trillion to build a new digital infrastructure to train and run forthcoming AI models with faster connections between complex IT system of chips, software, servers, and networking (Waters 2024).

The industry is growing so rapidly that countries with hyperscale data centers now host an International Data Center Day each March. The event is run by 7 × 24 Exchange International, an industry-funded association in Staten Island, New York. The event targets elementary, secondary, and tertiary schools to get young people thinking about careers in this fast-growing industry.

Wrap Up

Digitization is front and center in business today. When Harvard Professor Shoshana Zuboff released her award-winning book, The Age of Surveillance Capitalism (2019), she accurately foresaw a new business model in the making based on data collection and microtargeting described earlier. Now that our whole lives are searchable, what's next?

With generative AI fervor gripping Silicon Valley and Wall Street, hunger for greater computing capacity will most likely continue to surge in the second quarter of the 21st century. Imagine what the future holds to power an increasingly fast and expansive digitized world, a topic ripe for vigorous debate and discussion.

There will always be something new. On July 19, 2024, as this textbook went to print, the world experienced the largest global digital infrastructure outage in history, shutting down eight million PCs, laptops, servers, and other IT equipment running Microsoft Windows (Financial Times 2024). The insurance industry projected insurance losses upward of $1 billion for the thousands of claims due to the outage.

The digital failure was caused by Texas-based CrowdStrike (est. 2011), the world's biggest cyber security company that is hired by 29,000 global customers to protect their computer systems. The outage occurred when CrowdStrike was updating its Falcon Sensor software, which had not been properly vetted. CrowdStrike immediately apologized to its customers from banks to brokerages, airports, trains, hospitals, retailers, television stations, and more in Europe, Asia, and the United States.

This event highlights the interconnected nature of software ecosystems today. It also reminds us of the potential value of studying modern-day digitization so that you can use this information to the benefit of your business activities.

CHAPTER 11

Marketing

With digitization an explosive new reality, we now explore how marketers are responding.

The digitization functional area, discussed in Chapter 10, has opened up a whole new vista for marketers. Digitization is the mechanism used by advertisers to not only get potential customer's attention but also change human behavior, ideas, and attitudes within a targeted consumer group.

Successful marketers are astute observers of human behavior. They are skillful researchers, as demonstrated by the breakthroughs in data collection and analysis. Marketers are quick to adapt to new business environments such as the one we are living in now. There is a lot we can learn from marketers.

People in sales, advertising, merchandising, and public relations also spend their budgets judiciously. They realize that the marketing *functional area of business* is critical to the overall success of a business. All eyes are on them.

Earlier, we defined business as an organization, comprised of people who produce goods and services to sell for a profit to be distributed to stakeholders. The marketing functional area of business fits squarely into the **selling** part of our definition. If you are interested in sales and advertising, this is the functional area to pursue.

What Is a Business?
An organization
comprised of people
who produce goods and services
to sell
to earn a profit
distributed to stakeholders

Being levelheaded, practical people, marketers see the external world in the binary: that which they cannot control and that which they can control. Examples of external environmental factors that marketers realize they cannot control include the business cycle, global capitalism, scientific inventions, and population demographics. To invest money in these elements is not smart in the minds of marketers.

In contrast, elements that marketers believe they have a shot at controlling are worth time, effort, and money. In 1960, University of Notre Dame Professor Jerome McCarthy came up with a catchy way to remember such controllable elements, dubbed the Four Ps: **product, place, price,** and **promotion** (McCarthy 1960).

McCarthy's topology treated the marketing functional area of business as a management science to help executives better understand consumer behavior. The Four Ps compressed the marketing process into a memorable construct and remains in our business lexicon 60-plus years later, a tribute to Professor McCarthy's deep knowledge of this field of study.

Below, we examine the four marketing Ps with the aim of describing each element, exploring how the elements are changing in the 2020s, and considering how the Four Ps impact your buying habits and decision making.

Element #1: Product

To begin with, the marketing department is charged with designing a strategy that encompasses marketing activities and programs that will support the business's intended end goals for a specified period of time. This strategy includes the first of the Four Ps: **Product**. Businesses must determine what products they are going to sell. They must consider ways to differentiate their products from those sold by competitors. They will make every effort to attract customers in a highly competitive business environment.

Marketers consider, for example, who are the biggest buyers in society: women or men? What is your guess? If you guessed women, you could be on the brink of a successful career as a marketer. Women purchase between 70 and 80 percent of all goods and services in the U.S. economy.

Therefore, to be effective as a marketer, it is vital that you get into the minds and hearts of women; we buy the most stuff. Think about your moms who most likely bought your clothes, your food, your school supplies, your toothpaste, your sheets and towels, the furniture and appliances in your home, and much more. Women are famous for the amount of shopping done on Black Friday, the day after Thanksgiving. The marketers who came up with that blockbuster idea must be proud as this is one of the biggest commercial days in the United States.

The next question for marketers was how to get men to shop more. Marketers thus invented a day called Cyber Monday, the Monday after Thanksgiving, which aims to get men to shop online, a very clever strategy that has proven to be quite successful.

The Chinese have taken note of the success of Black Friday and Cyber Monday and, in 2016, created *Singles Day* to get single people to shop online. Singles Day falls on the 11th of November (11.11) and is now the busiest shopping day in China.

This tremendous marketing success led to Chinese businesses expanding their targeted customers beyond single people to include all online shoppers in the People's Republic of China. The result is a new **11.11 Global Shopping Festival**. Alibaba ecommerce giant rang up sales of $156 billion on November 11, 2023, the most ever spent in one 24-hour period anywhere on earth!

On the 11th of November each year, shopping becomes a sport and a form of entertainment in China. Why would Alibaba go to such extremes to promote its 11.11 Global Shopping Festival? Because marketers know that the **product** element requires consideration of not only the tangible goods that customers may buy but also the intangible allure associated with specific products.

We have all been tempted to buy things not necessarily because of the actual product itself, but because of its appeal to our sensibilities, preferences, and dreams. That is why Alibaba paid handsomely to include Nicole Kidman in their first 11.11 Global Shopping Festival, knowing how many women admire this world-renowned actor's consumer taste and lifestyle. The allure of a movie star became the **product** Alibaba presented to its consumers in the hopes that they would be tempted to buy its tangible online products as a result.

Tim Wu, Columbia University law professor and marketing expert, has studied ways that so-called attention brokers have effectively convinced us to view a **product** as more than meets the eye. Think about the notions of convenience and efficiency that have been marketed to consumers since the mid-20th century as valuable commodities. Buying a washer and dryer makes life easier. So does a microwave oven, automatic locks on car doors, and motion-detecting lights. Now that everybody has access to such products, Wu argues that 21st-century products are marketed to us as ways to express our *individuality*, a newly prized product in a world of mass-marketing.

As the marketer's notion of **product** became increasingly abstracted from the tangible product itself, the whole concept of **brand** exploded. It used to be that particular items that businesses manufactured and sold became brands, such as Hamburger Helper or Kleenex. The Ad Men of the 20th century helped businesses differentiate what they were selling from the glut of other products available for consumption. Nowadays, anything can be a brand when imbued with meaning such as a lifestyle brand (marketing a way of being) or a brand face (the way consumers see themselves while eating, wearing, and/or using a product).

Advertiser Dan Pallotta summarized branding in the *Harvard Business Review* as follows: "Brand is much more than a name or a logo. Brand is everything, and everything is brand" (2011, 150). In this way, our notion of the **product** marketing element takes new form and goes well beyond the notion of product differentiation.

Element #2: Place

Once you have established what you are selling, the next step is to consider where and how you are going to distribute your products to people who might be willing to buy what you are selling? There are many ways to think about this second marketing P called **place**, and the strategies being tried are unlike anything we have seen before in the world of marketing.

One of the biggest changes in place-based marketing is the rapid growth of ecommerce, which impacts the retail, logistics, manufacturing, robotics, and marketing industries. The largest e-commerce firms by revenue in 2024 were as follows:

- **Amazon**, founded in 1996 in the United States
- **JD.com** (Jingdong), founded in 1998 in China
- **Alibaba**, founded in 1999 in China
- **Pinduoduo**, founded in 2015 in China
- **Meituan**, founded in 2010 in China

Ecommerce firms are a direct challenge to retail merchandising as people no longer exclusively associate shopping with stores and malls. Walmart, once queen of U.S. retailing, turned to China's Tencent and JD.com to provide the necessary infrastructure to support ecommerce (e.g., cargo planes, drones, voice assistants, cloud computing, retail stores, online stores, social media, and epayment systems) as it switched from instore to online sales. The system is working for Walmart: sales in the first quarter of 2024 were up due to (a) more high-income customers shopping at Walmart online and (b) more in-store and pick-up sales.

Geographical Place

Place-based marketing has several layers, from geographical to psychological, physical, and digital. Let's begin with *geographical* place. As the world becomes more interconnected through rapid advancements in global capitalism, businesses can find customers across the six major inhabited continents. Learning how to navigate this global arena is tricky and can be expensive.

An early adopter of geographic place-based marketing was the Kellogg Company. In February 2012, the Michigan-based business purchased Pringles potato chips from Ohio-based Proctor & Gamble (P&G) for $2.7 billion in cash. Why?

Kellogg's wanted a direct route to selling its cereals outside the United States. Kellogg's CEO John Bryant announced that "Selling cereal and selling snacks are two entirely different skills, it turns out. When it comes to overseas snacks, Kellogg's currently lacks chops. What the company is buying in Pringles isn't just a line of products that is already hugely international, but a group of P&G merchandisers with the snack mind set" (Segal 2012). The job of the staff at Pringles was to geographically place Kellogg's products in foreign countries.

For this reason, Kellogg's decided to retain the people who worked in P&G's Pringles advertising department after the buyout because they possessed the requisite skills to take Kellogg's

global. Eleven years later, in 2023, Kellogg's split into two publicly traded business, one for cereals (e.g., Fruit Loops, Frosted
Flakes, Special K) and the other for salty snacks (called Kella-
nova, maker of Pringles, Cheez-Its, Pop-Tarts, etc.). Their products are sold in 180 countries today.

With M&As on the rebound in 2024, the large family-owned
confectionery company, Mars, expressed interest in buying Kel-
lanova for $35.9 billion in August 2024 to add more salty snacks
to its portfolio of candy, petcare hospitals, Wrigley chewing gum,
and the London-based Hotel Chocolat. Like Kellogg's, Mars is
making a play for what marketers call *brand affinity* around the
globe, including Africa and Latin America.

Psychological Place

A second layer of **place** is *psychological*. Marketers who study
psychology find novel ways to influence how and what people
will buy. If potential customers can be made to feel good or have
a positive association with a particular product, they are more
inclined to spend money on that product. Think about Alibaba's
hiring actor Nicole Kidman to launch its now famous 11.11
Global Shopping Festival.

Physical Place

Another layer of **place** is *physical,* the one most commonly
associated with retail shopping. Where do you physically place
your products in a store? Do you want your products to be on
full view at the end of an aisle? Do you want specific lighting
directly above your display? Do you want displays near or on the
self-checkout counters? Are you willing to pay more to personally set up a display of your products in a store rather than leave
it up to the store clerks?

Some businesses have taken the physical space concept to
another level, whereby stores have been re-created as recreational

spaces to encourage customers to play with new products for fun. Have you been to an Apple store or a Microsoft store where hard selling to customers takes a back seat to inviting customers to play with the new devices? Have you ever gone to a virtual store on gaming platform Roblox? If so, you know that marketers do not have a product to sell you. Rather, Roblox has created a way for retailers (e.g., Ikea, H&M, and Walmart) to meet young consumers—who keep opting out of targeted ads—in the hope that fun, immersive gaming experiences may build goodwill with prospective consumers. Roblox calls this "3D simulation communication," another example of physical **place**-based marketing strategies that link brand building with entertainment.

Lady Gaga, the world-renowned musician, songwriter, performer, actor, producer, business woman, and media mogul, rocked the world with one of the first big *virtual* **place-based** marketing strategies upon creation of her Lady Gaga virtual community of fans. As described on her site, *www.littlemonsters.com*, Gaga announced to her millions of fans that she would be choosing a select group of 10,000 super fans each year who get one-stop-shopping for all things Gaga. The idea has been a resounding success, taking place-based marketing to new heights.

Digital Place

Last but not least of the **place** element is *digital* marketing, which is revolutionizing the world of business today, thanks to the advent of sensors (on products) and beacons (in stores) that connect marketers directly with their products and their customers 24/7 (via mobile devices).

Tiny computer chips and sensors are installed on manufactured items that enable a business to track a product from the factory to the store and to the end consumer. This is called the Internet of Things (IoT).

If a customer purchases an Amazon Dash Button for $4.99 and adheres it to a household item, the customer need only press the button and the product is automatically reordered through Amazon Prime and mailed to the customer's home.

The sensors on the packaging of soft drinks and soap power, for example, detect where a product is bought and used, and when to reorder the product.

Most products purchased today contain a tiny, nearly invisible microchip (i.e., a "tag" or "transponder") that identifies a specific item and can transmit and receive signals. For example, each can of Diet Coke contains a microchip that was installed in the factory. Athletic wear contains a microchip that collects medical vital signs data from the wearer's body (e.g., heart rate, pulse). Each of these tiny chips has a unique identifier, which marketers call an *electronic product code* (EPC), a globally unique number that identifies that specific item.

EPCs are read using radio frequency identification (RFID) technology. According to the National Institute for Standards and Technology at the U.S. Department of Commerce in Washington, DC:

RFID is a form of automatic identification and data capture technology that uses electric or magnetic fields at radio frequencies to transmit information. An RFID system can be used to identify many types of objects, such as manufactured goods, animals, and people. Each object that needs to be identified has a small object known as an RFID tag affixed to it or embedded within it. The tag has a unique identifier and may optionally hold additional information about the object (2007).

In-store retailers install wireless RFID reader devices in every aisle that beam out electromagnetic energy (i.e., radio waves) to scan the microchips embedded in products as well as customers' mobile devices. Tag-reader communication enables retailers to track how long a person walks through a store, how much time is spent in each aisle, and what products shoppers pick up.

The value of the data collected through product microchip sensors and in-store beacons is the equivalent to a person's internet browsing history, as it reveals a great deal about personal preferences and shopping habits. Retailers also know where you are when you make purchases and can send you advertisements and coupons while you are standing in the aisle of a store, thinking about whether or not to make a purchase. If you decide not to purchase the item you were looking at, be prepared to receive text messages as you head home, enticing you to reconsider making that purchase.

Retailers use RFID technology to determine the contents of a shopping cart without having to physically scan each item. In this case, shoppers do not have to go through check-out lines. Instead, the readers scan the tagged items and charge the customer directly. The easiest way to do this is to have the customer download the retailer's app, allowing items to be charged through their mobile device for any items in their shopping cart upon exiting the store.

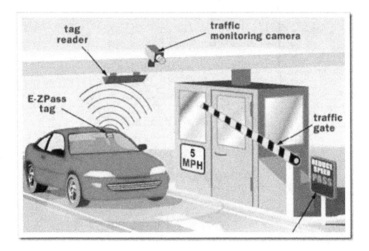

The new reader system is similar to how drivers are automatically billed when they go through a toll booth if the car has an E-ZPass tag on the windshield.

Advancements in **place**-based marketing reflect a whole new approach to customers, merchandising, and sales. The focus is now on *personalized selling on an industrial scale*. Consider, for instance, a flight attendant congratulating you on reaching 100,000 air miles while at the same time apologizing for the delay of your flight to Washington, DC, last week, offering you a complimentary gin and tonic—the same drink you had on last week's delayed flight—as a courtesy.

How did the flight attendant know this information about you and your travels? Airlines have a trove of traveler data on seat assignments, birthdays, credit cards, and the number of times a customer researched a flight on its app or website before booking. Airlines are hoping to use these data to boost profits and mitigate against growing agitation associated with shrinking leg room, narrower seats, fees for luggage, no free food service, and lengthy airport check-ins. Will having a friendly flight attendant—with a handheld device that contains your personal information—reach out to you personally make you feel valued? Or better yet, might it entice you to book another flight with this airline?

> Successful marketers are astute observers of human behavior. They are skillful researchers, as demonstrated by the breakthroughs in big data collection and analysis. Marketers are also quick to adapt to new business environments.

Advertisers in industries such as airlines have learned to use new technology to provide better services for customers and improve the bottom line. Their experiences can serve as lessons for all of us in business.

Element #3: Price

Historically, merchandisers established the prices for products using the laws of supply and demand. In the economics canon, general equilibrium theory teaches that the profit-maximizing **price** is where the aggregate demand curve for a product crosses the aggregate supply curve. Marketers knew not to price products so high that customers would be tempted to buy elsewhere, nor too low (i.e., below the firm's direct and indirect costs). Prices were then customized to accommodate the seasonality of a product, inventories, weather, location, and preferences of potential customers.

Once again, we see that digitization and sophisticated computer-generated algorithms are changing business models. Today, marketers value customer data more than the **price** a person is willing to pay for a product. As the Silicon Valley adage reveals, if you are not paying for a product, you are the product, meaning the value of your personal data exceeds the cost of the service provided. Thus, price may be the amount of money a person is willing to pay for a product or service. But price also may represent intangibles that a person is willing to give up, such as time, effort, quality, and personal data.

So how do marketers price their products? With the rapid dissemination of in-store beacons that connect with the microchip sensors installed on products that connect wirelessly with customers' mobile devices, merchandisers have their answer.

Computer scientists envision the day when marketers will no longer display prices on items. Instead, while a customer is standing in the grocery store aisle, marketers will send a digital message to a customer's mobile device with a personalized price for a product based on the value of a person's shopping history data online and offline. Updating price tags will go from being a daily physical in-store ritual to a continuous computerized ritual conducted through AI. Customers will not even know what other shoppers pay for the same product.

Such geofencing systems represent a concerted effort to attract retailers into shopping centers, knowing the mall has state-of-the-art wireless tracking hardware and software, viewed as a necessary part of marketing these days.

Ecommerce, digitization, beacons, microchips, handheld mobile devices, and geofencing are revolutionizing the **price** element of marketing in ways Professor Jerome McCarthy could never have envisioned in the 1960s!

Element #4: Promotion and Public Relations

The fourth marketing P is **promotion**. This is a vital piece of the marketing environment that focuses on advertising, publicity, propaganda, ad campaigns, personalized selling, sales promotions, and ultimately protecting the face of a business.

At present, marketers commonly refer to the fourth element as public relations (PR) because the concept of product promotion has expanded significantly over the past 60 years. As a result, executives no longer hold the job title of vice president for promotion, but rather vice president for public relations, vice president for public affairs, director of communications, or chief customer officer to reflect an integrated marketing strategy that blends the Four Ps together.

The **promotion** person is responsible for selling not only business products but also the business entity itself. They play the vital role as the public face of a business. No wonder, PR executives are among the highest paid people in the for-profit business sector.

The Ad Men and Ad Women

Sophisticated advertising has its roots in the 1920s on Madison Avenue in New York City, where some of the big industries of the U.S. Industrial Revolution and post–World War II boom hired a nascent group of merchandisers called the *Ad Men*. Two pioneers were Edward Bernays and Albert Lasker, who fundamentally changed the orientation of merchandisers.

Edward Bernays was one of the most influential pioneers in the field of promotion. Born in Vienna, Austria, as the nephew of Sigmund Freud, Bernays came to the United States to begin a career in marketing while in his 20s. His first book, Bernays (1923), put him on the map. He challenged conventional ideas and persuaded marketers to mold opinions held by the growing working class (Ewen 1996).

Bernays's ideas stuck and landed him on the cover of *LIFE* magazine as one of the 100 most influential Americans of the 20th century. Edward Bernays loved his work so much that he continued as a PR consultant almost until the day he died, at the age of 104. Had Bernays been born a hundred years later, he would have recognized that digitization is the new mechanism used by social marketers, whose aim is to change human behavior, ideas, and attitudes of a targeted consumer group through in-depth research and data collection (Kotler and Zaltman 1971).

In addition to reading the works of Edward Bernays, anyone serious about becoming a public relations expert would benefit from studying the life's work of **Albert Lasker**. A contemporary of Bernays, Lasker changed commerce in the United States in the first half of the 20th century with a host of creative PR strategies delivered on behalf of his corporate customers as president of the famed Lord & Thomas advertising agency. Jeffrey Cruikshank and Arthur Schultz's book about Albert Lasker, *The Man Who Sold America: The Amazing (But True!) Story of Albert D. Lasker and the Creation of the Advertising Century*, aptly sums up the life of this famous PR man (2010).

The brilliance of Lasker can be found in the array of public relations strategies he designed to promote and sell products that U.S. businesses were manufacturing at an industrial scale never seen before, ready for purchase by the rapidly growing middle class. Lasker's Ad Men promoted the quest of business entities to replace Ma-and-Pa sole proprietors with nationwide retail chains, something we take for granted today. Lasker taught TV viewers to accept commercials in return for free entertainment, a precondition for digital platforms today.

Lasker had his hand in a host of pathbreaking campaigns that resulted in the creation of the fourth marketing P, **promotion**, which now includes PR. In his own words,

> I was connected with the first advertising ever done on canned pork and beans, canned soup, canned spaghetti. When I with my associates conceived and financed the first advertising of tires; when I was of that group who first advertised automobiles; when with associates I defined advertising so that it became a force of social good to introduce to the people new and better ways of life, I could work inspired, because I was fulfilling myself (Cruikshank and Schultz 2010, 346–347).

Lasker amassed a great fortune and lived to see a new age in advertising. In 1942, this larger-than-life giant of PR closed the Lord & Thomas advertising agency and transferred his creative genius into promoting charitable causes he and his wife Mary admired. By the end of his life, Lasker—the original social marketer—was able to do something of "significance," in his own estimation, through advocacy and philanthropy.

While the Ad Men were rocking Madison Avenue, the **Ad Women** were making their mark on Fifth Avenue in New York City, the height of high fashion and retail. Three notable women made significant inroads by focusing expressly on the newfound independence of female shoppers and so-called "shopgirls" who worked in retail. The business acumen of **Hortense Odlum** led Bonwit Teller into an icon of the uniquely female universe of glamorous department stores in the 1930s. Her pioneering approach to retail influenced the retail models at other department stores owned by R.H. Macy, Edward Filene, and the Bloomingdale brothers.

Dorothy Shaver elevated Lord & Taylor into the legendary department store that embodied high fashion during World War II, earning an unheard-of-salary for a woman in retail of $1.5 million in today's dollars. And **Geraldine Stutz** of Henri

Bendel reinvented the look of the modern department store in the 1960s that lives on today in the lucrative world of fashion and retail.

To learn more about these pioneering businesswomen, see *When Women Ran Fifth Avenue: Glamour and Power at the Dawn of American Fashion* by Julie Satow who writes:

> The history of Hortense, Dorothy, and Geraldine has been overlooked, but while they were establishing their lives and careers decades ago, their experiences remain immediate and relevant, their challenges shockingly familiar. These were strong, complex women, figures with interlocking yet varying fates, pioneers of their eras whose efforts contributed to the contours of American fashion and helped pave the way for women today (2024, xxi).

Wrap Up

The famed Ad Men and Ad Women changed the way people understood the world. How will you use the tools offered through sales, advertising, merchandising, and public relations to make your mark on the world? How will you use your new skills and knowledge to promote your version of a profitable business?

CHAPTER 12

Management

This primer has focused on the fundamental building blocks of business, including legal structures, growth strategies, options for going global, entrepreneurship, small business development, equity and debt financing, digitization, marketing, and public relations. We have covered a lot of material with the intention of grounding you in the key facets of starting and running a business.

Now we come to our last functional area of business: management. I saved management for last because you already know something about this topic. We considered, for example, marketing skills that will enable you to manage your own careers in business. You understand the financial management steps necessary for those of you who go into finance. And you have your own experiences working with managers in paid jobs or volunteer service, during which you were able to observe bosses in action. Therefore, you will be able to approach this last functional area of business with some understanding of what management entails.

What Is a Business?
An organization
comprised of people
who produce goods and services
to sell
to earn a profit
distributed to stakeholders

Management fits into our definition of business through the **people** who comprise a business. If you are good with people, you may want to consider a career in management.

Ultimately, management is about power, which explains why the topic is so intriguing and why there are many books written about managers. Managerial power is key to business success in that it enables you to influence people and their decisions.

Power enables you to develop strategies you want to see implemented. Power enables you to hire the best people. Power enables you to motivate your staff. Power enables you to be a role model for others. Power enables you to harness the necessary resources to achieve your goals. Managerial power will enable you to make the changes you want to see in the world.

> Managerial power is key to business success
> in that it enables you to influence
> people and their decisions.

The Economist magazine, a venerated business publication, has a weekly column devoted exclusively to management titled "Bartleby: Labour of Love." When first launched, the publication recognized that "The modern economy has been immensely complex. Coordinating the production of goods and services across international supply chains represents a huge achievement. Management at all levels is probably more difficult today than ever before. This seems an ideal moment to launch our new column" (2018:57). The column continues to be published each week to the interest of its readership.

Our examination of management in this primer is threefold. First, we will define management. Second, we will examine the job of a manager. Third, we will explore what people will expect of you when you become a manager.

What Is Management?

Simply put, *management is the process of coordinating resources to achieve the organization's goals*. Sounds simple, right? Let's break down that definition into its component parts to see what is actually involved.

Management is a **process**, meaning there are no clear steps I can offer you as to how to manage. Each situation, each manufacturing process, each client interaction, each human resource interface, each financial instrument, each industry, each logistical component, each data process, and each problem requires a manager to deal with a unique situation. Moreover, the management process is ongoing; there is no clear beginning, middle, and end.

Management is a process of **coordinating** all the functional areas of the firm. That's a big job. Managers are constantly juggling pieces, a skill that requires multitasking. Are you someone who can multitask? Or are you someone who likes to be given one task to accomplish at a time? Effective managers tend to be those who can juggle many pieces of the business simultaneously, using critical thinking skills to prioritize.

What are managers coordinating? **Resources**, that is, all types of resources required to meet the needs of a particular business at a point in time. Economists group resources into three categories to include land (i.e., physical spaces, property), labor (i.e., human resources, people), and capital (i.e., tangible, financial).

In the end, management is the process of coordinating resources **to achieve a specified goal**. Just because a manager is busy all day, making decisions, securing resources, mobilizing people, analyzing data, and coordinating activities does not mean the manager will be deemed successful. The key to success in management is achieving an agreed-upon goal. This is how you will be judged as a manager and how your year-end bonus will be determined. Before you accept a job as a manager, be sure to ask for clarity on the specific goal(s) you will be expected to achieve in the end.

Managerial Functions

The entire premise of this primer is to expose you to what businesspeople call the *functional areas of business*, the key domains that every businessperson needs to understand to be successful. Now we are going to look at what managers do all day, which in business is called "management functions." Try not to confuse these two terms—*functional areas of business* and *management functions*—as they have distinct meanings.

You get a job as a manager. Great! What are you going to be doing all day? A French mining engineer named Henri Fayol in 1888 labeled the primary functions of management as planning, organizing, commanding, coordinating, and controlling. Today, businesspeople have compressed Fayol's topology into four key management functions to suit the contemporary business environment of the 2020s: **planning, organizing, monitoring, and leading/following**, discussed in turn as follows.

Planning

We defined management as a process of coordinating resources to achieve a goal. The planning function suggests that we start planning based on the last part of the definition: the ultimate goal. Whatever plans we devise depend on what it means to successfully achieve the stated goal of the business.

Planning requires acute *strategic* formulation. A strategic business planner might ask:

- What would make our business unique?
- How could we outperform our competitors?
- What does success look like?
- What does effectiveness look like?
- How can our business play to its strengths?

- How can our business products and services be distinctive?
- What risks are worth taking and not taking?

To achieve its goals, a business must devise plans, be they strategic, tactical, or operational. *Strategic plans* are the most comprehensive type of plan and do not include details on how the business is going to achieve its goals. Rather, strategic plans present a big picture of what the business wants to look like in five-plus years.

Tactical plans present some of the nuts and bolts required to achieve the big picture as articulated in the strategic plan. Tactical plans encompass what needs to occur within a one- to five-year window and are presented on a smaller scale than strategic plans, and thus are easier to periodically update as new information feeds into the system.

Operational plans are the most flexible because they address very specific aspects of a strategic plan that can be achieved in the short term (i.e., within one year) to help the business achieve its broad strategic objectives.

Organizing

Once the strategists have clarified their vision, managers charged with the organizing function go into action mode to put the plans in place. Their focus is on how to achieve the goals efficiently and effectively. Organizational managers must think about the who, what, when, where, how, and how much.

In other words, organizational managers begin to identify and coordinate the pieces of the managerial process necessary to reach the firm's goals.

Monitoring

Monitoring entails overseeing the various moving parts required to put a business plan into action. Managers who assume this function are charged with assessing the degree to which the business is reaching its operational, tactical, and ultimately strategic plans. Are people doing their parts? Are there sufficient resources? Is there enough money? Do we have to make operational changes? What kinds of corrective action are advised? Are we getting closer to our goals?

In the 19th and 20th centuries, managers associated the monitoring function with "controlling," which is certainly one way to manage a process. In the 21st century, however, managers learned that controlling can lead to micromanagement and other adverse outcomes that do not always bode well for the managerial process. The concept of controlling has thus been expanded to a discussion of how to monitor ongoing activities in ways that yield the best results for the business. How you monitor the business process will most likely be unique to your style, workplace, occupation, and industry.

Leading/Following

The last of the four managerial functions is leading/following, two sides of the same coin. To be an effective leader, one must learn how to follow. Conversely, effective followers need to know how to lead. In business, we realize that there is only one CEO. Most of our time will be spent learning how to be good followers in anticipation of the day when we might be asked to lead.

Managers assuming the leadership function are charged with finding the most effective ways to motivate people to do whatever is within a staff member's means to help the business achieve its stated goals. Can you find ways as a manager to match people's skills and interests with the tasks at hand? Can you find ways to keep people satisfied and productive? Can you discover what people want to contribute to the business and then secure the necessary resources to make that happen? If so, you will contribute to the overall goals of this business.

At colleges today, there is a big push to host leadership training programs often for academic credit. It is great to be able to assume leadership with confidence and skill. However, do not be in such a hurry to leave a position in which you are very skilled to assume a supervisory position until you are ready. As the saying goes in the trades: *you may lose a good plumber and gain a lousy manager.* Think about how many times that has probably happened!

The Roles of Managers

The abovementioned managerial functions indicate what managers are doing all day: planning, organizing, monitoring, and leading. Now we take a look at what people will expect of you as a manager, something we call the roles of managers of which there are three: **informational, interpersonal,** and **decisional roles**, described in turn as follows.

Informational Role

Being able to put your finger on information that will help your business succeed is critical to success. Managers assuming the informational role are charged with gathering pertinent data. What do you need to know to achieve your stated goals? Where do you get good information? What is your data reconnaissance method?

Gathering information is an ongoing task for a manager. As such, it is key to read as much as you can to keep abreast of the latest in your industry and occupation, to talk to people willing to help you access relevant information, and to seek out timely information both internally in your business and in the broader business community.

Once collected, a manager then discerns what to do with the collected information. To whom should the data be disseminated? Who would benefit from having specific information? Does everyone in your business need to know everything? What is urgent? What information is not urgent?

Depending on your industry, there may be *formal* channels people rely upon to obtain needed information to do their jobs. Business managers may choose staff meetings or digital messages as formal dissemination mechanisms. The choice is up to you as the manager depending on what seems to work best with your staff.

An *informal* way to collect and disseminate information is around the water cooler (or coffee pot) where people tend to gather and chat. Informal information can be just as valuable to a business as formal information. What is your style? What kinds of information collection and dissemination techniques have you observed on the job? What has worked? What information have you wished your manager had shared that might enable you to do your job better? If you are not getting adequate information, let your supervisor know. It can make a big difference in the degree to which you will be productive on the job.

Now that white collar workplaces have veered toward more online work, managers have new challenges. It is not as easy to access information about what's happening on the ground when people are not actually on the ground. As you try out your management skills, take into account ways that you can feel confident you are tapping into the reality of your workforce, including those who work remotely.

Interpersonal Role

Effective management starts with you understanding yourself. Who are you? What makes you unique? What are your preferences? What do you demand of others? Self-awareness enhances our ability as managers and is learned through examination of our own values, emotional intelligence, cognition skills, adaptability, and personalities. Having a good sense of yourself is necessary to be effective with others.

A manager then branches out into the interpersonal, meaning the interaction between people in the workplace, yourself included. This is key to succeed as a manager. Being a liaison between people requires learning *supportive communication techniques* to understand a given situation and the people involved. Skillful communication leads to personal agency (or control), the empowerment of colleagues, enhanced relationships, and an energized workplace where people can be productive.

Communication skills are twofold. First one learns to develop strong listening skills, whereby people feel truly heard by you as their manager. This entails focusing the mind on what the person in front of you is trying to communicate without distraction. Effecting listening requires being quiet and not talking. This is not easy or automatic but can be developed with practice and in time. Second, effective communication requires one to learn supportive speaking techniques that empower you and your colleagues.

When employed effectively, supportive communication results in people being able to express their ideas with confidence to engender openness and trust in the workplace. Supportive communication also can be used to correct behaviors, deliver negative feedback, or point out someone's shortcoming. The overall goal is to enhance the interpersonal relationships within the workplace—through supportive listening and speaking—while tackling whatever difficult issue needs to be discussed.

Try to be cognizant of the many ways interpersonal communication has been disrupted by digitized workplaces and off-site work. Videoconference calls, for example, do not always bring out the best in people, nor does it allow everyone to participate in meaningful ways. It is your duty as a manager to recalibrate online conversations, which are distinct from face-to-face conversations

Managers may also be asked to play an interpersonal role outside their business, say in the community. This entails participating in community events as a figurehead for your business. Think of ribbon-cutting ceremonies, heralding the opening of a new building or a new community center where the chief executive of a business has a pair of scissors in hand to cut the ribbon for the camera. External interpersonal managerial skills are just as important as internal interpersonal skills.

Decisional Role

The last role managers may be asked to play is the decisional role. This is when a person has been granted authority to make decisions for the business that will impact how successfully a business achieves its goals.

A fancy title, however, does not always come with decision-making authority. Often in my work in the Arab world, I have seen highly educated women with important looking titles who, in reality, had little to no power. They were never given any authority to make decisions. Thus, it might be valuable to look below the surface of your culture to see who gets to make decisions. Whether you are being asked to be a manager or are joining a new business, find out who the decision makers are and who will be able to help you succeed.

The three managerial roles—informational, interpersonal, and decisional—are interconnected. A manager vested with authority over an organizational unit is granted status that leads to the kinds of interpersonal relations that provide access to information that enables the manager to make strategic decisions. Thus, while you may be asked to wear one of the managerial hats, over time you may see yourself wearing all three.

Wrap Up

Management, the process of coordinating resources to achieve a goal, is a challenging but potentially rewarding job. The challenge goes beyond knowing how to establish plans, secure financial resources, design a production process, and working endless hours every day. Management requires adroit skills in communicating with people, be they members of the board of directors, suppliers, financiers, subcontractors, employees, customers, and/or the general public. Perhaps, the skills learned to be an effective manager may spill over into your personal life and serve you in additional ways.

Hence, my recommendation is to take courses in human development, psychology, and management in college before you start a career in business. If you are smart, hardworking, and inquisitive, you will probably be tapped to become a manager or supervisor someday, at which time these managerial skills and knowledge will serve you well.

Bibliography

Bernays, E. 1923. *Crystallizing Public Opinion.* New York, NY: Boni and Leveright.

Cruikshank, J.L. and A.W. Schultz. 2010. *The Man Who Sold America: The Amazing (But True!) Story of Albert D. Lasker and the Creation of the Advertising Century.* Boston, MA: Harvard Business Review.

Einstein, M. 2016. *Black Ops Advertising: Native Ads, Content Marketing, and the Covert World of the Digital Sell.* New York, NY: OR Books.

Ewen, S. 1996. *PR! A Social History of Spin.* New York, NY: Basic.

Financial Times (FT). July 20–21, 2024. "Experts Pick Over the Wreckage After IT Failure." 7.

Financial Times (FT). June 25, 2024. "Apple Accused of Breaking EU Rules on Fair Competition." 10.

Ford, H. 1926. *Today and Tomorrow.* New York, NY: Productivity Press.

Franchise Direct. 2024. "Top 100 Global Franchises 2024." www.franchisedirect.com/top100globalfranchises/rankings.

Gartner. 2024. "Gartner's 2024 Annual Report on Cloud Computing." www.gartner.com/en/products/special-reports.

Hodgson, C. August 19, 2024. "Big Tech Groups Suck up Precious Water Reserves in Virginia's 'Data Centre Alley'." *Financial Times.*

Kotler, P. and G. Zaltman. July 1971. "Social Marketing: An Approach to Planned Social Change." *Journal of Marketing* 35: 3–12.

Levintova, H. June 2022. "The Smash-and-Grab Economy." *Mother Jones*: 15–9.

McCarthy, E.J. 1960. *Basic Marketing: A Managerial Approach.* Homewood, IL: R.D. Irwin.

Pallotta, D. June 15, 2011. "A Logo Is Not a Brand." Boston, MA: Harvard Business Review. https://hbr.org/2011/06/a-logo-is-not-a-brand.

Ruehl, M. June 26, 2024. "Singapore Is Well Placed to Benefit From the Rose of AI Data Centres." *Financial Times.*

Sataw, J. 2024. *When Women Ran Fifth Avenue: Glamour and Power at the Dawn of American Fashion.* New York, NY: Doubleday.

Schamotta, J. February 13, 2024. "How Much Data Does Your Car Log?" Comparitech. www.comparitech.com/blog/information-security/how-much-data-does-your-car-log/.

Schlossber, J. March 1, 2024. "How RFID Technology Is Changing the Retail Industry in 2024." *Progressive Grocer.*

Segal, D. April 21, 2012. "When a Sugar High Isn't Enough." *The New York Times.* BU:1.

Shenkar, O. 2010. *Copycats: How Smart Companies Use Imitation to Gain a Strategic Edge.* Boston, MA: Harvard Business Press.

Small Business Administration (SBA). 2024. www.sba.gov.

Spencer S. May 16, 2021. "Inventor of the Glue That Makes Post-it-Notes Stick, Dies." *The New York Times.* 29.

Tau, B. 2024. *Means of Control: How the Hidden Alliance of Tech and Government Is Creating a New America Surveillance State.* New York, NY: Crown.

The Economist. June 20, 2024. "Cyber-Security: Wiz Kid." 52.

The Economist. May 18, 2024. "Retail: Through the Floor." 58.

The Economist. April 20, 2024. "Was It All a Dream? Why the Stockmarket Is Disappearing." 59.

The Economist. January 27, 2024. "Private Markets: In for a Trillion." 60–2.

The Economist. September 14, 2019. "Chips With Everything." 13.

The Economist. January 6, 2018. "The Year of the Incumbent." 49.

The Economist. May 26, 2018. "Our New Column on Management and Work." 57.

United Nations Conference on Trade and Development. 2024. *World Investment Report.* New York, NY: United Nations.

U.S. Department of Commerce and National Institute of Standards and Technology. April 2007. *Guidelines for Securing Radio Frequency Identification (RFID) Systems.* Special Publication 800–98.

U.S. Department of Labor. Bureau of Labor Statistics. 2024. North American Industry Classification System (NAICS). www.census.gov/eos/www/naics/.

U.S. Internal Revenue Services (IRS). n.d. *"Statistics of Income Bulletins."* www.IRS.gov/taxstats.

Wall Street Journal. February 16, 2018. "Regulator Targets Firms With Dual-Class Shares." B1.

Waters, R. June 22–23, 2024. "Artificial Intelligence: The Nvidia Supremacy." *Financial Times.*

Witt, S. December 4, 2023. "The Chosen Chip: How Nvidia Is Powering the A.I. Revolution." *The New Yorker.*

Zuboff, S. 2019. *The Age of Surveillance Capitalism: The Fight for a Human Future at the New Frontier of Power.* New York, NY: PublicAffairs.

About the Author

Patrice Flynn is an author, Fulbright Research Scholar, and Distinguished University Professor at Mount St. Mary's University (est. 1808). She has taught global business and economics at Johns Hopkins University, the U.S. Pentagon, George Washington University, and now the Mount, where she received the Richards Award for Teaching Excellence. Her research across five continents examines global capitalism, labor markets, civil society, and China's New Silk Road. Previous positions include Vice President for Research at Independent Sector, Senior Vice President for Administration and Finance at Effat University, and CEO of Flynn Research, during which time she was selected as one of Lifetime Television's Women of the Year.

Index